Super Graphs, Venns, & Glyphs

Hundreds of Great Data Collecting Activities to Build Real-Life Math Skills

by
**Honi Bamberger and
Patricia Hughes**

SCHOLASTIC
PROFESSIONAL BOOKS

New York • Toronto • London • Auckland • Sydney

Acknowledgments

In writing this book we realized that some of the terrific ideas came from our friends and colleagues at New Hampshire Estates Elementary School and Oakview Elementary School, both in Silver Spring, Maryland. We give special thanks to: Maura Backenstoe, Stephanie Bamberger, Gail Ceccarelli, Sharon Cohen, Rebecca Sincevich Dearman, Stephanie Flynn, Cybele Gagne, Ellen Levine, and Chris Perretti, whose endless excitement and interest in mathematics spirited them to collect, represent, and analyze data about things that really mattered to their students.

Cover design by Jaime Lucero and Vincent Ceci
Cover photograph by Donelly Marks
Interior design by Jaime Lucero and Robert Dominguez / GrafiCo
Interior photographs by Honi Bamberger and Patricia Hughes
Interior illustrations by Maxie Chambliss and Vincent Ceci

ISBN # 0-590-67477-3
Copyright © 1995 by Honi Bamberger and Patricia Hughes
All rights reserved.
Printed in the U.S.A.

12 11 10 9 8 7 6 5 4 3 2 1   1 2 3 4 5 6 / 9

Table of Contents

Table of Contents

Introduction

We have found that youngsters who participate actively in collecting, displaying, and discussing data about themselves have a deeper understanding of the math embedded in these projects. Whether it's a graph of the transportation students took to get to school that morning ("bus, train, car, other") or a lunch box glyph showing children's favorite foods ("hot dog, spaghetti, pizza, ice cream"), hands-on activities make math come alive for young learners.

For many years, we have been leading conference sessions and conducting in-service workshops teachers throughout the country. Our goal was to encourage educators to make data collection a part of students' daily lives. As we conducted those sessions, we kept in mind the 1989 Standards of the National Council of Teachers of Mathematics (NCTM), which points to society's need for a population that can analyze and interpret data, and use the results to make informed decisions.

In our conversations with teachers, we found that many recognized the need to help students meet that goal. In fact, teachers were enthusiastic and eager to implement our ideas. At times, though, questions arose. "How and when during the school year do I get started?" "Which activities would be most appropriate for primary-age youngsters?"

"What materials will I need?" "How do I guide the conversations when the graphs, Venn diagrams, or glyphs are complete?" What the teachers wanted, we realized, were specific ideas, activities, and models for implementing data collection in their own classrooms. "Write a book," someone suggested at the end of a workshop.

Graphs, Venns, and Glyphs is meant to inspire teachers to collect data with their students every day. There are enough ideas to include data collection as morning activities, as part of reading, social studies, and science units, or as holiday-related projects at any time of day.

About the Authors

From 1989 to 1995 the authors were involved in a research study funded by the National Science Foundation. Through Project IMPACT (Increasing the Mathematical Power of All Children and Teachers), a collaborative effort between the University of Maryland at College Park and the Montgomery County Public School system, we studied the effect of how providing in-service training to teachers affects their teaching of mathematics. We interacted with teachers daily, giving demonstration lessons at times. During the year, teachers were supported as they made changes in the way they taught and experimented with new activities and approaches. We encouraged teachers to use a constructivist approach, which emphasized concept development in which children would be actively engaged in the mathematics learning process. Children would construct their own understandings and mathematical procedures.

Honi J. Bamberger, a former full-time classroom teacher, was one of three principal investigators from the University of Maryland who worked, from the onset of the project, with the teachers of Project IMPACT. She was a mathematics specialist offering ongoing support and teacher training to the teachers in the research study. She worked daily with teachers to generate ideas for implementing the NCTM Standards in their classrooms and encouraged the use of daily data collecting as a means for increasing the amount of time that teachers spent on mathematics. She is currently an associate research scientist at the Center for Social Organization of Schools at Johns Hopkins University.

One of the classroom teachers who implemented Project IMPACT strategies was Patti Hughes. At the time she worked with a class of second graders, a group with a diverse student population. She was looking for a way to expand the opening of each school day to include a form of data collection. A daily graph seemed a possibility. Each morning, as part of the children's early routine, the youngsters participated in such an activity, from clipping their vote on a clothespin graph to placing their picture in the appropriate ring of a Venn diagram. The children's enthusiasm for these projects reinforced for Patti the power of this tool.

Book's Organization

The format of the book is as follows: In Chapter 1 we provide the rationale for data collection in the classroom, showing how such activities correlate to NCTM standards and to other curriculum areas. In Chapter 2 we suggest how to construct a variety of graphs, Venn diagrams, and glyphs (pictures that convey information), including the materials needed along with basic directions. Chapter 3 focuses on special graphs that will surely excite your students, from clothespin graphs to string

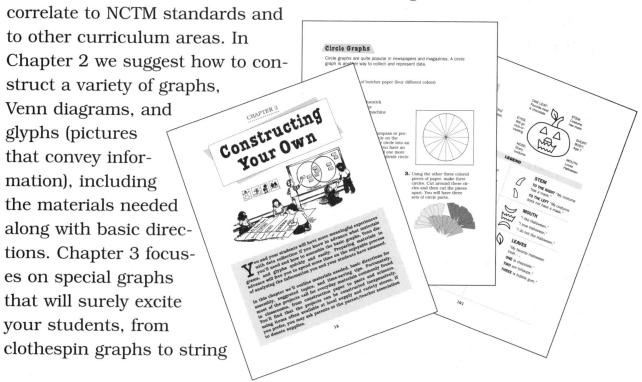

graphs. In Chapter 4 you will find sample lessons for graph-making in reading, social studies, and science, as well as in math. We focus on Venn diagrams in Chapter 5. There we offer a sample lesson on how to introduce Venn diagrams to your students and how to make two-ring and three-ring Venns with connections to a variety of topics, such as food and weather. And finally, Chapter 6 explains exactly what glyphs are, shows how to introduce them to your class, and gives directions for making class-pleasers such as Turkey glyphs or Lunch box glyphs.

Finally, in the appendix you'll find a basic materials supply list, different sizes of grid paper, various pictures, and other data organizers. You can photocopy and use these pages in your classroom.

Your Turn

The ideas in this book should be used as a springboard. You will find that you get your own ideas from our suggestions. These will surely be based on what you know about your own students, and may very well be more appropriate and motivating than activities we suggest.

Have fun! Make collecting and talking about data part of your daily conversations. You'll find that you can review math content that you've taught previously, encourage children to make and justify predictions, and motivate your students by posing questions that capture their curiosity.

CHAPTER 1

Why Teach Data Collection?

Open any newspaper, in any city, on any given day, and you will see that mathematics—data collection and graphing— is "alive and well." In *USA Today*, for example, bar graphs, line graphs, and circle graphs tell readers about trends in fashion, incomes of specific sports players, and which orange juice is the most popular.

Statistics are presented to the public all the time. Important decisions are based on those figures. The results of polls are used to make decisions about subjects as diverse as who will win the presidential election and which dry cereal children prefer. Surveys are taken frequently that help businesses make decisions about how best to advertise and which products and programs consumers will buy. A lengthy narrative may be difficult for the average citizen to read, but a graph—when created in a clear, straightforward manner—provides a simple presentation of information. In this way the reader is able to quickly gather information that may help make a decision.

A Real-Life Tool

Often, children learn mathematics in school and wonder when they will ever use the skill in real life. In fact, taking surveys, collecting data, and creating and interpreting graphs provide students with experiences in the classroom that parallel those in the real world. After all, children should know that scientists and other researchers collect data for experiments, people in business collect data to make decisions on the popularity of products they produce, and professional athletes look at their "stats," comparing current with past performance. And people in the construction business often create graphs to compare the cost and effectiveness of materials that they may use in construction projects.

For children to see the practical application of statistics they need frequent opportunities to collect data themselves. They also need to make decisions about the most effective ways to represent information and to interpret and analyze the results.

The National Council of Teachers of Mathematics (NCTM) Standards for Curriculum and Evaluation (1989) provide us with a vision of what school mathematics should be and what educators hope children will have learned about themselves and mathematics upon completion of school. Foremost is the goal that students will value mathematics and become confident in their ability to use it. We as educators hope that children will become mathematical problem solvers, able to communicate and reason mathematically.

Involving children in data collection provides teachers with a vehicle for accomplishing these goals. It works this way: A problem is established. Children need (or want) to find an answer. ("Let's find out who we think will win the Super Bowl.") Students communicate with one another and decide upon a method for collecting the information. Then they come up with an appropriate way to represent it in an easy-to-read manner. Once the data has been displayed, children may work together to analyze it. In this way, youngsters work cooperatively on a math-related issue. Not only is this educational, it's also fun!

Data collection activities reinforce writing as well as math. The observations that children make can be recorded in math journals. Youngsters can use their journals to write about how they decided to represent their data or what strategy they used to collect it. Math journals can also be used to collect ideas for future data collection activities ("Next time I want to find out what juice the kids drink for breakfast").

Data collection activities provide children with chances to communicate both orally and in writing, and to justify their statements. And it allows teachers to make constant connections between various subjects areas and mathe-  matics and between different mathematics concepts. Best of all, data collection need not be limited to a "unit" in mathematics, but rather to real school activities, such as taking the attendance or discussing Thursday's schedule.

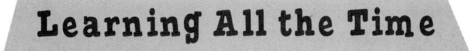

Learning All the Time

The NCTM Curriculum and Evaluation Standards for School Mathematics explain that, "Children's questions about the physical world can often be answered by collecting and analyzing data. After generating questions, they decide what information is appropriate and how it can be collected, displayed, and interpreted to answer their questions" (p. 54). It is for this reason that we create graphs, Venns, and glyphs in our classrooms. Not only are students motivated to answer the questions, they are curious to see how their classmates respond. In addition, they happily anticipate, even predict, what the next day's activity will be. There is every reason to think that your students will react the same way.

CHAPTER 2

Constructing Your Own

You and your students will have more meaningful experiences with data collection if you know in advance what materials you'll need and how to assemble the basic graphs, Venn diagrams, and glyphs quickly and easily. Preparing materials in advance will free you to spend more time on the enjoyable process of analyzing the information you and your students have amassed.

In this chapter we'll outline materials needed, basic directions for assembly, suggested topics, and time-saving tips. Fortunately, most of the projects call for everyday materials commonly found in classrooms, from construction paper to paste and scissors. You'll find that the projects can be constructed inexpensively, using items often available at local supply and variety stores. If you prefer, you may ask parents or the parent/teacher association to donate supplies.

Graphs

Bar Graphs

A bar graph is a simple, straightforward way to introduce children to collecting and representing data.

MATERIALS

- large sheet of poster board
- yardstick or meterstick
- markers
- Velcro
- index cards (various colors, one card per student; plus extra cards)
- optional: laminating machine

DIRECTIONS

1. You may construct your bar graph vertically or horizontally. Use a yardstick and markers to draw the lines. (If a laminating machine is available, laminate the poster board now.)

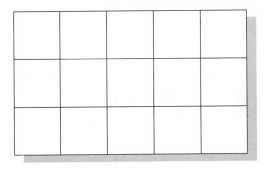 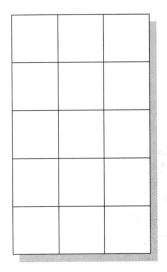

2. Add a small square of Velcro (loop side works nicely) to each box on the graph. Leave the first box of each row blank for now.

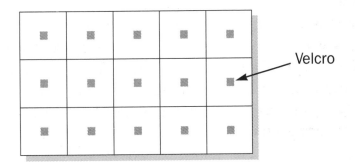

13

3. Write each child's name on an index card, one card per child. The cards should be a bit smaller than the boxes on the graph. Laminate before placing the other side (sticky side) of the Velcro on the backs.

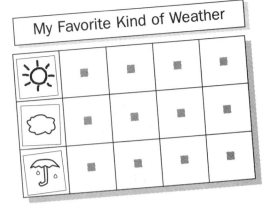

4. Hang the graph in an area that is accessible to all and where it can be seen by all for discussion.

5. Place pictures of the subject for each row (such as sun, cloud, umbrella, to indicate sunny, cloudy, or rainy) in the corresponding open squares.

Tips

- **Laminate all the materials for longer use.**
- **Use self-adhesive Velcro.**
- **Buy Velcro in bulk. Large quantities are available at craft stores.**
- **Instead of using index cards and Velcro, let children cast their votes using Post-it notes. They handle easily and can be purchased inexpensively at office supply stores.**

6. Discuss the meaning of the graph and ask students to place their name cards in the appropriate places.

Tips

- Use assorted colors for name cards, so children can interpret data based on colors as well as whatever is collected.

- On occasion, vary the shape of the name cards. Make a set of cards for each child using circles, squares, triangles, rectangles, and ovals. Shapes can factor into the analysis of the data.

- On occasion, use photographs of the students in place of their name cards.

- Assign a child to remove the name cards at the end of each day.

- Store name cards in resealable plastic bags or storage bins near the graph.

- Use portfolios and/or underbed storage boxes to keep graphs organized and easily accessible.

- Change your graph monthly, so you and your children stay interested.

SUGGESTED TOPICS

- What is your favorite ice cream?
- How did you get to school today?
- Which school lunch tastes best?

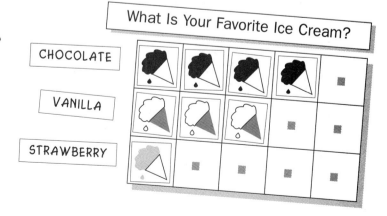

15

Bar Graph With Colored Strips

This type of graph is similar to the bar graph, except colored strips of paper are used in place of children's name cards.

MATERIALS

- poster board (4 different colored sheets)
- Velcro
- markers (permanent and wipe off)
- yardstick or meterstick
- optional: laminating machine

DIRECTIONS

1. On one sheet of the poster board draw lines like this:

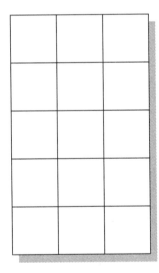

2. Use the other three colors to cut out a class set of strips to fit in the spaces on the actual graph.

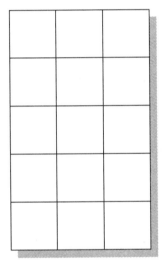

Remember to make enough for each child to have one of each color. For example, if you have 30 children you would need 90 strips (30 yellow, 30 red, 30 blue). If possible, laminate the graph and the strips.

3. Place a small square of Velcro (loop side) onto the graph. Put one piece in each section of the graph.

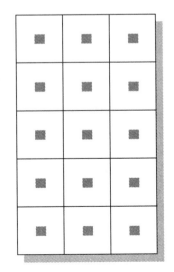

16

4. Use the opposite side of the Velcro (sticky side) to place small squares on each colored strip.

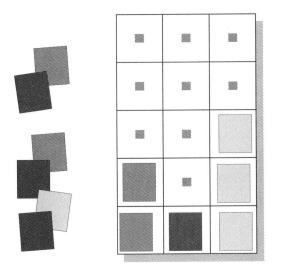

5. Create a legend, using the three different strip colors, that looks similar to this:

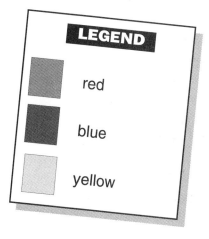

Explain, or review, how to use the legend.

6. Have children consult the legend and record their choices on the graph. Discuss. Wipe off major categories at the end of each day.

Tips

- To create the legend, use pieces of the actual colored strips.
- For a visually pleasing graph, use bars (strips) composed of four colors that work well together.
- When children first use this graph they tend to place their cards anywhere on the graph. (Sometimes there are spaces between cards.) If this happens, discuss ways to organize the information in a manner in which it can be interpreted more easily.

SUGGESTED TOPICS

- Which animal do you like best? Cat, dog, horse.

- Which "special" class do you enjoy most? Art, music, physical education.

- I'd rather take a ride on a: . . . plane, boat, train.

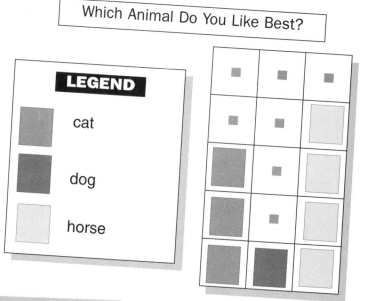

Graphs With Real Objects

These graphs use concrete objects, such as shoes or cookies.

MATERIALS

- choose one from below:
  - ✔ shower curtain liner
  - ✔ drop cloth or oil cloth
  - ✔ window shade
  - ✔ bulletin board paper
- masking tape (may be colored)
- optional: laminating machine

DIRECTIONS

1. Lay the liner on the floor.

2. Use the masking tape to place lines. If you used the bulletin board paper, laminate it now, if possible.

3. Place actual objects directly on the graph. For example, if you made a graph called "What Kind of Shoes Are You Wearing Today?" children would place a sneaker, a shoe with a Velcro closure, or a shoe with laces, in the appropriate row.

- Place the graph on a large open space (such as the floor or school yard) where all can see it.
- Store your graph by folding it a few times, or roll it up.

SUGGESTED TOPICS

- Which cookie would you rather eat? (Children choose from three plates of cookies.)

- What type of hat are you wearing?

- What flavor milk do you like best? (Use empty milk cartons covered with construction-paper labels to indicate chocolate, strawberry, etc.)

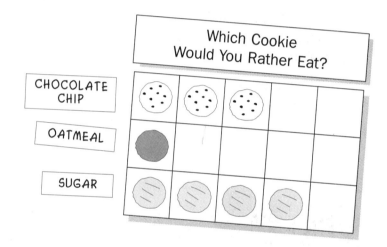

Clothespin Graphs

A clothespin graph is a fun way to generate data. It works best when children are given only two choices.

MATERIALS

- poster board (two different colors)
- assorted colored clothespins (wooden or plastic)
- permanent markers
- dot-shaped adhesive labels
- optional: laminating machine

DIRECTIONS

1. Cut the poster board in half lengthwise.

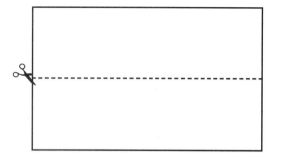

2. Tape two halves together, one of each color, such as red and blue. It should look something like this:

3. Number the left side and the right side. Put an adhesive dot beside each number. This will help children place their clothespins. Laminate, if possible.

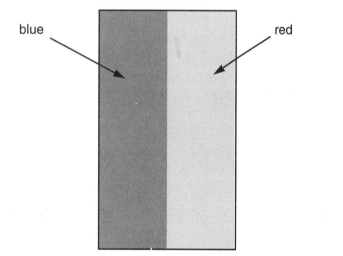

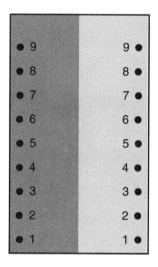

4. Review the topic of the graph and let children cast their votes.

Tips

- Create a color pattern using the dots (red, blue, red, blue, and so forth).
- Let children choose a different colored clothespin each day.
- Store the clothespins in a small basket.

SUGGESTED TOPICS

- Which type of recess do you prefer? Indoor or outdoor.

- Which team will win the Superbowl?

- In our school, I think we have more: boys, girls.

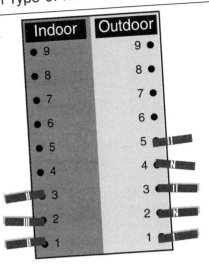

Which Type of Recess Do You Prefer?

Rectangle Graphs

Rectangle graphs are wonderful for a unit on fractions. They are an excellent way to show equal parts of a whole.

MATERIALS

- poster board
- paper clips
- assorted colors of construction paper (cut into strips)
- permanent markers
- wipe-off markers
- optional: laminating machine

DIRECTIONS

1. Determine the number of people that will be using the graph. (Don't forget to include yourself!)

2. Cut the poster board in half horizontally. Tape along the edge so it becomes a long horizontal piece. It should look like this:

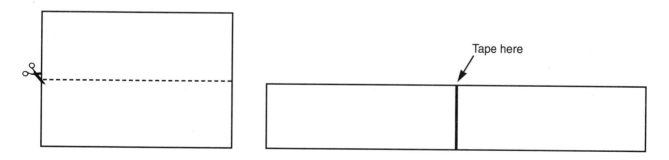

Tape here

3. Use the marker to draw vertical lines of equal width. Make sure to have the same number of strips as people using the graph. Laminate, if possible.

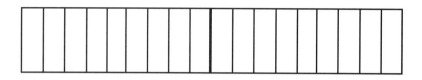

4. Choose three different colored pieces of paper. Cut strips about the same size as the strips on the graph. Cut enough for every child in each color. (Example: 30 children = 30 red, 30 blue, 30 yellow.)

5. Create a legend using the three colors of paper. Laminate, if possible. It should look something like this:

6. In the center of each strip on the graph, place a paper clip. Ask the children to cast their votes by sliding their colored strip right under the paper clip.

 **Tip**

■ The first time the children use this graph they may put their strips up in any order. If this happens, discuss whether there is another way to group the strips that might make it easier to interpret the graph. (Students may suggest sorting the strips by color.)

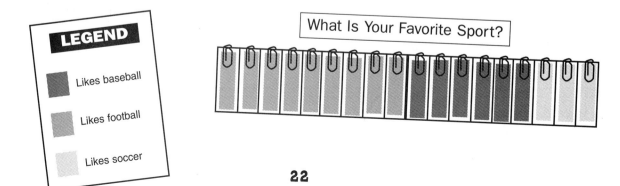

Circle Graphs

Circle graphs are quite popular in newspapers and magazines. A circle graph is another way to collect and represent data.

MATERIALS

- assorted sheets of butcher paper (four different colors)
- scissors
- wipe-off markers
- heavy tagboard
- rubber cement or gluestick
- compass or protractor
- optional: laminating machine

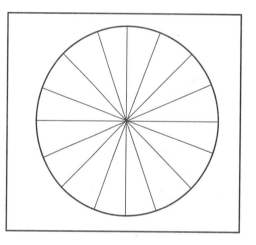

DIRECTIONS

1. Using markers and a compass or protractor, draw a large circle on the butcher paper. Divide the circle into an even number of parts. If you have an odd number of people, add one more part. (Example: 27 people, divide circle into 28 parts.)

2. Cut around the outside of the circle only. Leave the inside pieces intact. This will be the circle graph on which children will place their votes.

3. Using the other three colored pieces of paper, make three circles. Cut around these circles and then cut the pieces apart. You will have three sets of circle parts.

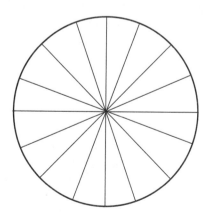

4. Use the rubber cement to paste tagboard to the circle pieces. (The paper pieces will not hold up for long without the tagboard.) If possible, laminate the basic graph as well as all the pieces.

5. Lay the circle graph out in front of you. Cut Velcro into small pieces. Place one side of Velcro (loop side) on each piece on the graph. You may need to use two small pieces of Velcro—one for the narrower section, the other for the wider section of the circle. You will need more of the sticky side of the Velcro than the loop. Be prepared—you'll have leftovers!

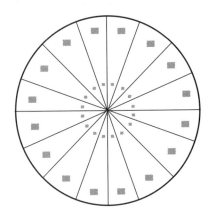

6. Now place the other side of the Velcro (sticky side) onto your circle pieces. You will need to place the Velcro on the same part of the piece as the circle graph. Try to come as close as possible. Keep the Velcro in the same place for all the pieces. This part takes patience!

7. Design a legend for the graph using the three colored pieces. This is where your choices can be written. For example, for a circle graph on Favorite Lunchtime Foods, blue means "I like spaghetti," green means "I like pizza," purple means "I like hamburgers." Laminate, if possible.

Favorite Lunchtime Foods

LEGEND
- Spaghetti
- Pizza
- Hamburger

SUGGESTED TOPICS

- Which school lunch would you rather eat? Meatballs and spaghetti, fish sticks, pizza.

- How many hours do you spend reading each week? Less than 1, 2–5, more than 5.

- Where would you rather spend your summer vacation? Home, camp, farm, other.

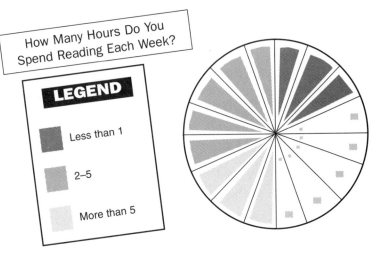

How Many Hours Do You Spend Reading Each Week?

LEGEND
- Less than 1
- 2–5
- More than 5

Venn Diagrams

Venn diagrams engage your students in higher order thinking. They are able to compare and contrast two concepts, ideas, or characters. Venn diagrams can be used across the curriculum. They offer a clear visual for representation and comparison of data.

Two-Ring Venns

MATERIALS

- large sheet of butcher paper
- large chalkboard compass or
  long piece of string tied to a piece of chalk
- colored index cards or Post-it notes
- Velcro
- markers
- oaktag sentence strips
- scissors
- optional: laminating machine

DIRECTIONS

1. Lay out the large sheet of paper. Use the chalkboard compass or string and chalk to draw two large rings. They need to overlap so there is an area shared by the two rings.

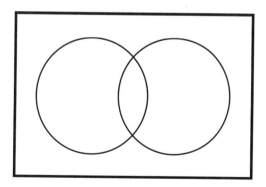

2. Use a marker to trace over the chalk lines from the circle. Laminate the paper, if possible.

3. Cut the Velcro in small pieces. Randomly place pieces of the loop side onto the Venn diagram. Make sure to place pieces inside the circles, within the intersection, and outside the circles as well.

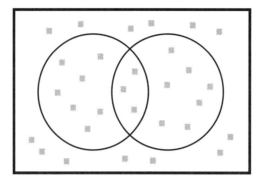

4. Write the children's names on small colored index cards. Laminate these, if possible. Then place the small pieces of the sticky side of the Velcro on the backs of the name cards.

5. Use sentence strips to label each circle. Remember to place the Venn diagram in a place where all can see and take part.

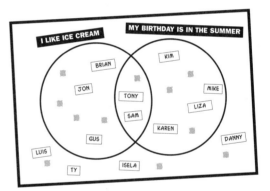

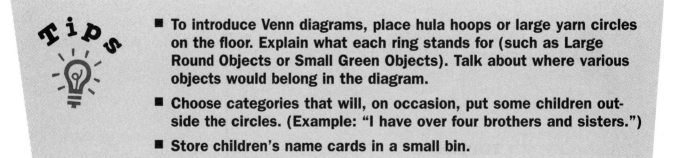

- To introduce Venn diagrams, place hula hoops or large yarn circles on the floor. Explain what each ring stands for (such as Large Round Objects or Small Green Objects). Talk about where various objects would belong in the diagram.
- Choose categories that will, on occasion, put some children outside the circles. (Example: "I have over four brothers and sisters.")
- Store children's name cards in a small bin.

SUGGESTED TOPICS

- I am a boy. I am a girl.

- I like to eat ice cream. My birthday is in the summer.

- My age is an even number. I have been to the beach.

Three-Ring Venns

Three-ring Venns should be used after children are comfortable with the two-ring Venns.

MATERIALS

- butcher block paper
- large chalkboard compass or long piece of string tied to a piece of chalk
- index cards, various colors
- Velcro
- markers
- scissors

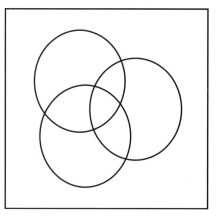

DIRECTIONS

1. Follow the same steps used for the two-ring Venn diagram, but include a third ring. Be sure to leave spaces in the intersections of the circles.

2. Make name cards for each child. Place Velcro on the backs. Be sure to put Velcro directly on the diagram as well.

 **Tip**

■ Reinforce children's concept of a three-ring Venn diagram by placing three overlapping large hula hoops or large yarn circles on the floor. Discuss what the rings represent and where various objects would belong.

SUGGESTED TOPICS

- I am in the first grade. I like to eat pizza. I have a sister.

- I love cold weather. My name has more vowels than consonants. My phone number begins with "9."

- I have my driver's license. I live in a townhouse. I have a brother.

Glyphs

Glyphs teach children to consult a legend, follow directions, and convey information about themselves. Glyphs are decorative and add lively, educational objects to your bulletin boards and walls. Children like to discuss what the glyphs tell about the artists who made them.

MATERIALS

For most glyphs you will need:
- construction paper, various colors
- scissors
- paste or glue
- crayons or markers
- optional: laminating machine

DIRECTIONS

In Chapter 6 you will find specific instructions for making a range of glyphs, from Books to Umbrellas. In general, though, the steps are as follows:

1. Post a legend indicating what various features mean. (For example, an umbrella handle that turns left means "I have two siblings" while a handle that turns right means "I have more than two siblings.")

2. Have students create individual glyphs according to that legend.

3. Display the finished pieces, and discuss.

CHAPTER 3

Special Graphs

Many classroom teachers who do graphing on a regular basis look for novel ways to display the data that their students collect. Using a variety of graphs seems to create enthusiasm in both students and teachers. It also enables children to transfer their understandings to different formats. Children gain a great deal of confidence knowing that they are able to use and interpret data from many different mediums. In this chapter you'll find some novel ways to collect and discuss data in your classroom.

Bottle Graphs

A bottle graph is one in which children cast their votes by pouring a standard amount of water into the bottle that represents their choice. When all participants have cast their votes, children look at the levels of the water in the various bottles to see which is the highest (it got the most votes), the lowest (it got the fewest votes), and so on.

MATERIALS
- 4 clean, empty, clear bottles of the same size
  (Plastic 2-liter soda bottles work well.)
- measuring cup (half-cup)
- bucket of water
- funnel
- blue food coloring

DIRECTIONS

Ask the class to find out which is their favorite place to swim: the ocean, a lake, a swimming pool, or "other."

1. Set out four identical empty bottles. Label each bottle with a category, such as Ocean, Lake, Swimming pool, and Other.

2. Have children cast their votes, one at a time. Next, have them fill a measuring cup with water. Show them how to use the funnel to pour the water into the bottle of their choice.

3. Then ask children to analyze the data by looking at the height of the water in the bottles. The bottle with the most water is the favorite.

Children can then estimate how many people may have poured the water into the containers by doing a sampling of five to ten students and finding out who poured their water into each bottle. This smaller sample will act as a "benchmark," enabling students to come up with a fairly accurate estimate.

Older students might write about why they think the results turned out the way they did.

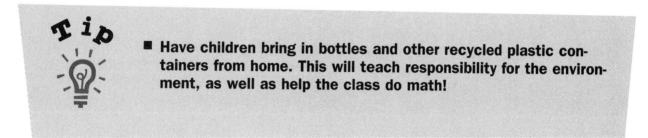

■ Have children bring in bottles and other recycled plastic containers from home. This will teach responsibility for the environment, as well as help the class do math!

SUGGESTED TOPICS

Bottle graphs can be used to collect data that answer these questions:

• Which is your favorite beverage? Juice—*use water with orange food coloring,* milk—*use water with an ounce of milk to make it cloudy,* soda pop—*use water with orange and blue food coloring to make it brown.*

• Where would you rather play with sand? Playground, beach, sandbox—*instead of water, have children fill the half-cup with sand and pour the sand into the two-liter bottles.*

• Which writing tool, if any, will sink in water—a marker, a pencil, or a jumbo crayon? Children fill a half-cup with colored water to cast their "vote." The height of the water indicates the answer. Once the data is analyzed, the children talk about how they will test their predictions.

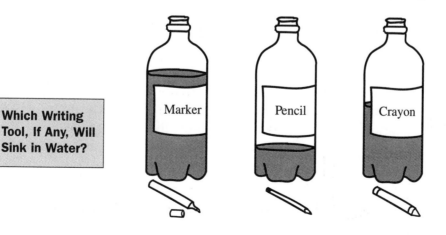

Which Writing Tool, If Any, Will Sink in Water?

Marker   Pencil   Crayon

Clothespin Graphs

With a clothespin graph, children cast their votes by placing a clothespin in the section that corresponds to their answer.

MATERIALS

- clothespins (wood or plastic)
- tagboard
- markers

DIRECTIONS

1. Using a marker, divide a piece of tagboard into two columns. Label one column Yes and the other column No.

2. Pose a question, such as: Do you read for at least 20 minutes each night?

3. Let children clip their clothespin in the place on the graph that corresponds to their answer.

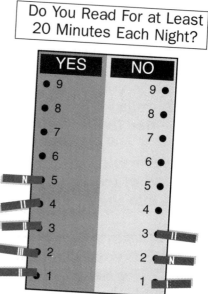

Do You Read For at Least 20 Minutes Each Night?

4. If you like, ask children to write their names on the clothespins so that, when data is analyzed, they can refer to voters by name.

Variation: Have children vote for their preference on an issue, such as I prefer to: sing a song, whistle a tune.

Tip

■ Students may place their clothespins randomly on the graph. If so, they may find it difficult to compare the number of votes in each column. To help them analyze their data more effectively, add numerals to each column on the graph. This will help children place their votes in one-to-one correspondence.

SUGGESTED TOPICS

Yes or No

- Do you like to read?
- Do you think the (name of the local baseball, basketball, hockey or football team) will win: tonight, tomorrow, Sunday?
- Can you run a mile without stopping?
- Are you able to do 25 sit-ups?
- Do you like to sing?
- Did you watch television last night?

- Did you like (name the story or book) that we just read?
- Would you like to be (name a character from history or from a book that you just finished reading)?
- Are you able to count by fives to 100?

- Do you eat at least one piece of fruit every day?
- Are you able to count by tens to 100?
- Can you ride a bicycle?

"I Prefer"

"I would rather" or "I prefer to":

- play baseball, read a story
- eat a taco, eat pizza
- go swimming, build a sand castle
- write with a pen, write with a marker
- watch baseball being played, play baseball
- go for a boat ride, go for a train ride
- bake cookies, bake bread
- bake cookies, eat cookies
- eat dinner at home, eat dinner in a restaurant
- listen to the radio, watch TV
- watch a video at home, go to the movie theater
- have indoor recess, have outdoor recess
- eat lunch in the cafeteria, eat lunch in the classroom
- grow flowers, grow vegetables

For older students, these questions can be followed up with a writing assignment, recorded in their math logs or on sheets of paper. For example, if students have responded to "Would you like to be _____ (person from history)," they can write their reasons.

Quantity Graphs

These graphs are typically large squares split into quadrants. They may be made out of felt, oaktag (tagboard), or plastic, or can be drawn with crayons on bulletin board paper or with chalk on the chalkboard. A label identifies the major question or issue (such as My Favorite Season) and each quadrant indicates the specific category (such as Summer, Fall, Winter, Spring). Children place their names or photographs in the quadrant of their choice.

In this type of graph there is no linear representation. Instead, the child often randomly places his/her name or photograph inside the quadrant. It is the quantity (often defined by the area taken up by the name tags or photographs), that provides the information for data analysis.

My Favorite Season

SPRING	SUMMER
KAREN LETY LORETTA JOE	ISELA LISA DANNY JO BRIAN MIKE LULU DAVID
AUTUMN	WINTER
JEREMY VICTOR RICK	BELINDA NORMA GENNY

Stacked Graphs

Here is a very different, but visual way to collect data and show the results of a survey: Create a graph in which objects stacked high in various categories indicate children's preferences, or "votes."

With a tuck of cardboard here and a bit of glue there, a milk carton can be transformed into a covered cube, excellent for casting a vote in this vertical graph. As milk cartons are stacked in various piles, children can tell—at a glance—which category got the most or least "votes."

MATERIALS

- empty, clean, cardboard milk containers
  (One-cup size work well.)
- construction paper
- paste or tape
- sentence strips
- markers or crayons

DIRECTIONS

1. Show children how to cover their milk container with construction paper and affix the paper with paste or tape.

2. Ask children to write their name on the container. (When youngsters discuss who voted for what, they can refer to the names on the cartons.)

3. Let children cast their votes by stacking their container in the pile with which they most closely agree.

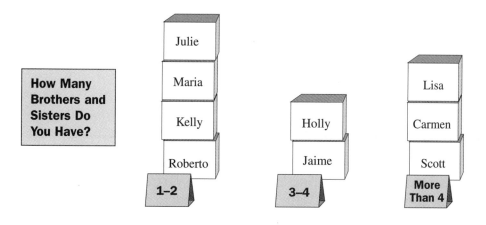

String Graphs

Children use string to indicate their answers. The length of the string indicates their response.

MATERIALS
- ball of string
- scissors
- tape

DIRECTIONS

1. Ask children to measure an object, such as the circumference of a pumpkin. Have them use scissors to cut the string to the exact circumference.

2. Children then suspend the string from a strip of masking tape which hangs horizontally across the wall, chalkboard, or bulletin board.

Interestingly, children often randomly place their string on this graph, with this possible result:

When asked to discuss the results of the data, they have a difficult time doing so. Often, without any teacher prompting, they make the decision to organize the strings so that they are in sequence from shortest to longest or from longest to shortest. Satisfied with this organization, they are then ready to discuss and draw inferences from the data.

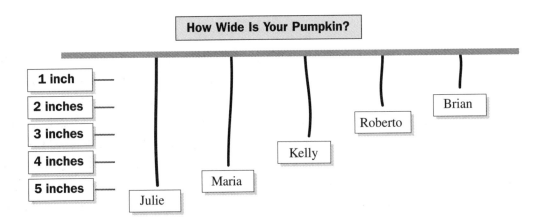

How Wide Is Your Pumpkin?

1 inch
2 inches
3 inches
4 inches
5 inches

Julie
Maria
Kelly
Roberto
Brian

Variations: Children measure their heights, the circumference of any part of their body, or the distance of their long jump.

CHAPTER 4

Graphs Everywhere

As we look through social studies and science books, we find that mathematics is used frequently, often expressed as tables and charts. We find information about areas such as how high a plant grew in a month, the distances from the sun to the planets in the solar system, and the dates, expressed in a time line, of major wars in United States history. Students need to learn how to read and interpret these charts. In doing so, they will come to appreciate how powerful they are in conveying information in an easy-to-read format.

Getting Started

You can help your students make use of these tools. The best way to start is by asking them to create graphs on subjects that have significance to their interests and everyday lives.

- Children are learning about dinosaurs. Some youngsters love the fierce T-Rex for its strength and courage. Others like the Brachiosaurus for its long neck. With these preferences in mind, ask the class to indicate their likes through a Favorite Dinosaur graph. Have them illustrate that animal and place it in the corresponding column on the graph. Then talk about which is the most popular.

- For a unit on transportation, ask children how they would rather travel on a trip: by car, by bus, or by train. They can place this information on the graph, then write about their choice.

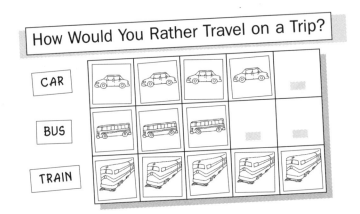

How Would You Rather Travel on a Trip?

CAR

BUS

TRAIN

- After an author or illustrator study on Donald Crews or Eric Carle, for example, let youngsters "vote" for their favorite book.

We've found that children are thinking and talking about these issues anyway. Collecting data about important issues poses authentic questions, and is a way to meaningfully integrate mathematics into their daily school lives.

On the following pages you will find seven lessons that can be used to integrate graph-making into many areas of the curriculum. To help you get started, we provide the materials needed, the directions, and possible teacher/student exchanges. The conversations are actual ones that took place in our classrooms. They show teaching strategies we used to encourage children to think on their own, and to work as part of a team. The exchanges in *your* classroom will reflect your students' thoughts and reactions.

Which Leo Lionni Story Did You Like Best?

We often begin the day by asking children to cast their votes about their "favorite things." Our students love coming into the classroom each morning to see what the graph of the day is. They even begin predicting what it might be the following day. By the time we ran out of ideas, the children had ideas of their own.

OVERVIEW

One such exercise was a survey of first graders following a week-long study of the works of author/illustrator Leo Lionni. (By the way, many Leo Lionni stories have mathematics themes and make excellent math-related literature selections.)

During that week, children heard Lionni's delightful stories. From Monday to Friday, teachers conducted language arts lessons based on themes from the books. Mathematics that was imbedded in the story was used as a springboard for the math lesson for that day. By the end of the week, the children had compared five different stories and were ready to decide which of the books they enjoyed most. Your class can create a graph based on an author/illustrator of your choice. Here's how:

MATERIALS

- file cards, about 3 x 5 inches
- crayons or markers
- large sheet of oaktag (for foundation of graph)
- paste or glue

DIRECTIONS

On file cards, ask children to draw a scene from the book that they liked the best, then paste their card on the horizontal picto-graph where it belongs.

MY FAVORITE STORY BY LEO LIONNI

Inch by Inch

Swimmy

Frederick

The Biggest House in the World

Fish is Fish

Teacher: Boys and girls, please look at the data that we collected today and let's use "think-pair-share."

Think-pair-share is an instructional strategy. It gives children time to actually process a question. We had children think for a "wait-time" of about ten seconds.

First, think of your answer. Now, tell a friend what you were thinking. (*The talk between students lasted about 45 seconds.*) Now think about what your friend has said. (*Another ten seconds.*) Who would like to share something that they heard or something that they were thinking?

Child: I was thinking that most children liked *Swimmy* the best.

Teacher: What makes you say that?

Child: It's got the most pictures.

Teacher: How did you know that there were the most?

Child: It's the longest one.

Teacher: Oh! So, you saw that the cards made the longest row. Did anyone else think that *Swimmy* was the book that the most people liked, but you knew that for a different reason?

Child: I knew it was the most because it's seven. Seven is more than five and *Frederick* has five.

Teacher: How did you know that *Swimmy* had seven and *Frederick* had five?

Child: I counted them.

Teacher: O.K. Who can say something else about the data that we collected?

Child: *Inch by Inch* and *The Biggest House in the World* are the same.

Teacher: What do you mean by "the same"?

Child: They are tied. They both have three.

Teacher: Oh, so they have an equal number of pictures. Who can say something else about the data that was collected?

Child: Hardly anybody liked *Fish Is Fish*.

Teacher: Why do you say that?

Child: Only two people drew pictures for that story. That's hardly anybody.

Teacher: Let's talk a little bit about why you think people liked certain stories more than others. Think about why you liked the story that you drew a picture about. What made you like that story more than the other ones? First "think" for about ten seconds about this question. (*Again, give the children this silent time to think. No hands should be up and no one talks.*) Now tell a friend what you were thinking about.

(*One minute.*) Now let's share a few of the reasons why you think some of these books are better liked than other ones.

Child: *Swimmy* had really pretty pictures. I think seven people liked that book because the pictures looked like sponge paintings. We made sponge paintings in art.

Child: Stories about mice are good. *Frederick* was better than *Fish Is Fish* because I didn't know that Frederick was really working. His friends were getting ready for winter, but I thought that Frederick was just playing. But, he wasn't. He really helped his friends when they were sad and tired of winter.

Child: I think a lot of people liked Frederick because he gave his friends surprises. I like to give my friends surprises too.

Child: *The Biggest House in the World* had really pretty colors and designs on the snail's shell.

(*This discussion went on for another ten minutes.*)

Teacher: Since all of the children in all of the first-grade classes read the same stories this week, and all of the classes were going to make graphs like this one, think about how you believe the graph made by Ms. McDowell's class might look. (*Ten seconds were given.*) Now talk with a friend about your answer.

The teacher got some suggestions from the children, asked them for their rationales, and invited them to compare their graph with that made by Ms. McDowell's class. The children were very eager to see how the two graphs compared.

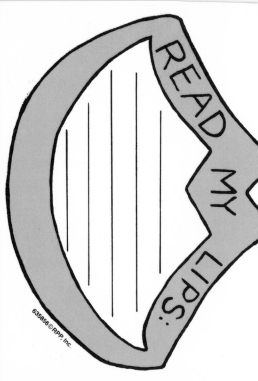

EXTENSIONS

With older students (end of first grade and beyo[n]
into many of the graphing activities. Children do
do a graph. A few days of the week they may us[e]
some observations. They might write:

• about why they made their choice
• their analysis of the data
• how they think the data might vary if it were c[o]
  time of year, on a different day, or in a differen[t]
  ent aged children.

One of the funniest stories occurred in a second-
children were graphing which was their favorite f[ ]
predicted that apples would be the favorite fruit,
to children at lunch time and it seemed pretty po[ ]
dren came in the morning they placed their nam[e]
show which was their favorite fruit and, surprisingly, only a few children
had placed their names beside the picture of the apple. When the teacher
told the children what she had predicted a student raised her hand.
"Everyone knows that second graders can't eat apples!" The teachers
seemed surprised and asked why not. The child smiled and pointed to the
spaces missing in her mouth and said, "Second graders don't have teeth!"

How Did You Get to School Today?

On the first day of school we have children at all grade levels graph their
means of transportation to school that day. In Kindergarten, the children's photographs are taken with a Polaroid camera. A piece of magnetic tape is adhered to the back. Pictures of a school bus, a child walking,
a car, and a bicycle are placed on a horizontal bar graph. Children are
told that this graph will show how they got to school today. They place
their picture on the graph where it belongs.

MATERIALS
• horizontal graph
• "instant" camera
• magnetic tape
• pictures, as described above
• Post-its and pencils (older children)
• optional: laminating machine

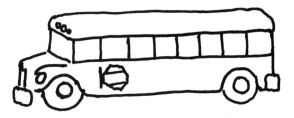

DIRECTIONS

In first grade, children's names are laminated onto file cards. Children are asked to find their names and think about their answers. They then place their names on the place on the graph where they think they belong.

Second-, third-, and fourth-grade children are asked to write their names on colored Post-its and place these on the graph.

Everyone, across the grades, is given time to do the graph. Then, along with the other "opening activities," the data is analyzed.

TEACHER/STUDENT EXCHANGE

We began by placing the graph in a spot where all of the children could see it.

Teacher: Boys and girls, I'd like you look at the graph for about 15 seconds and think of something that you can say about what you see. *(Tell the children not to raise their hands during this time but to just think of something to share.)* Quietly tell the person who is sitting next to you what you were thinking about. *(Give them time to whisper something to their neighbor. Then use some sort of a signal to get their attention. Clapping or ringing a bell work well.)* Who would like to share something that they were thinking about or something that they heard?

Child: Lots of people came to school by the school bus.

Teacher: Thank you for sharing that with us. Who would like to say something different?

Child: Only two children rode their bikes to school today.

Teacher: How do you know that?

Child: I counted.

Teacher: Would you come up to the graph and show us what you counted and how you counted?

Child: One, two. See, two children rode their bikes to school.

Teacher: Thank you. Did everyone see what _____ was sharing? Would someone share something different?

Child: More children came to school in a car than on a bike.

Teacher: How do you know that?

Child: Only two children rode their bike to school, but more than two children came by a car.

Teacher: How many children came in a car today?

Child: Seven.

Teacher: Would you show us how you know that it was seven?

Child: I counted. Two, four, six and one more makes seven.

Teacher: Oh, so you counted by two's to find out that there were seven. Did anyone use a different method?

Child: One, two, three, four, five, six, seven.

Teacher: So, you counted by ones to get to seven. What else can you say about today's graph?

Child: Most of the children walked to school today.

Teacher: Tell us how you know that.

Child: The walking part of the graph has more pictures than any of the other parts.

Teacher: So, you know that that means that most of the children walked. Who can figure out how many children walked? Take ten seconds of thinking time and see if you can figure out the answer. (*Again, give them time to think with no hands raised and no talking.*) Now whisper again to a friend what you think the answer is. (*Give them a chance to share their answers.*) Who would like to share with the whole class? (*We call on about six different children to say the answer out loud, even if they are saying the same things.*)

Child: Twelve

Child: Thirteen

Child: Twelve

Child: Fourteen

Child: Twelve

Child: Twelve

Teacher: I heard different answers. How can we know for sure what the right answer is? What could we do to check?

Child: We could count.

Teacher: O.K. How shall we count? We listened before and learned that there are different ways to count things.

Child: We could count like this: one, two, three, . . .

Teacher: Okay. _____ says that we could count by ones. Let's all count by ones together. Let's begin. One, two, three . . . twelve. So, what did we find out?

Child: There are twelve children who came to school by walking.

Teacher: Pat your head if you agree.

This analysis should continue for as long as interest is maintained. Once a routine has been established, daily data discussions should only last about 5 to 10 minutes (so they don't "cut into" other subject areas). Some teachers actually set a timer to limit the discussions. Once children are writing or drawing in their math logs (journals) on a regular basis they can write additional observations about the daily graph during their free time.

More Horizontal Graph Ideas

The following is a list of other topics, by grade level:

Grade One

- I am a girl. I am a boy.

- What color are your eyes? brown, blue, green, other

- My hair is long. My hair is short.

- Do you have a pet at home? yes or no

- Look at the shirt that you are wearing today. Does it have a pattern on it? yes or no

- What color is your hair? black, brown, blond, red, other

- What type of shirt are you wearing? long sleeved, short sleeved, sleeveless

- My shoes: have laces, have Velcro, are slip on

- My hair is: curly, straight, wavy, none of the above

- I would rather sleep on my: back, side, stomach

- What do you usually drink with your lunch? milk, juice, water, other

- Are you wearing a watch? yes or no

- How did you get to school? car, bus, bicycle, walk

- How many letters are in your first name? 0–3, 4–6, more than 6

- How many pockets are on your clothing? 0–2, 3–5, more than 5

- How many people live in your house? 0–3, 4–6, more than 6

- How many bedrooms are in your house? 0–2, 3–4, more than 4

- Which hand do you write with? left, right, both

- I like stories with: cars, people, animals

- On the weekend I would rather: play sports, go to a movie, relax

45

- What month were you born? January–April, May–August, September–December

- On what day of the month is your birthday? 1st–10th, 11th–20th, 21st–31st

- Which season is your birthday? spring, summer, fall, winter

- Where would you rather live? city, country, beach, mountains

- My age is: even, odd

- My house number is: even, odd

- What time did you go to bed last night? 7:30–8:30, 8:31–9:30, after 9:30

- What time did you get up this morning? before 7:00, between 7:00–8:00, after 8:00

- When I color I'd rather use: crayons, markers, colored pencils

- I'd rather take a ride on a: boat, train, plane

- I am the oldest child in my family. I am the youngest child in my family. I am the only child in my family. I am somewhere in the middle.

- I live in a: townhouse, apartment, house, mobile home, boat

- I have lost at least one tooth so far. I have not lost any teeth yet.

- My family has more boys. My family has more girls.

- I have fruit in my lunch today. I do not have fruit in my lunch today.

- I like when the weather is cold. I like when the weather is hot. I like when the weather is cool. I like when the weather is warm.

- The size of my shoes is: less than size 10, between 10–13, more than size 13

- I wear a watch. I do not wear a watch.

- I have my own library card. I do not have a library card.

- Someone else from my family goes to this school. I am the only person from my family who goes to this school.

- Count the total number of letters in your first and last names. Then write your complete name on a Post-it and write the total number of letters as well. Then place the Post-it on the graph where it belongs. (Should be intervals of 7: 1–7, 8–14, 15–21, more than 21.)

example:
Kim Yen Nguyen—12

- Suppose that A=1, B=2, C=3, D=1, E=2, F=3, G=1 . . . Z. Determine the special number of your first name. Write your name, the addition number sentence, and the total on a colored Post-it. Find the place on the graph where your name belongs. (Should be intervals of 5: 0–5, 6–10, 11–15, 16–20, more than 20.)

You can change the pattern every week to give children practice recognizing and extending patterns, adding, and using number sense to place their names where they belong.

example:
Peter Daly
1 + 2 + 2 + 2 + 3 = 10;
1 + 1 + 3 + 1 = 6;
10 + 6 = 16

- Think of the number that marks the place where you live. Determine the total of all of the digits. Write your name and the total on a Post-it. Place it on the graph where you think it belongs. (Should be intervals of 8: 1–8, 9–16, 17–24, 25–32, more than 32.)

example:
7207 Elm Street
Gordon—16

- Think of your telephone number. Determine the total of all seven digits. Write your name on a Post-it. Write the total on the Post-it. Place it on the graph where you think it belongs. (Should be intervals of 10. 1–10, 11–20, 21–30, 31–40, 41–50, more than 50.)

example:
555–2397
Jesse—36

• Write your first name. For each vowel you get 2 points. For each consonant you get 5 points. Figure out how many points you have altogether. Write your name and that number on a Post-it and place it on the graph where it belongs. (Should be intervals of 10: 0–10, 11–20, 21–30, 31–40, 41–50, more than 50.)

You can change the value assigned to vowels and consonants to give children practice with addition, number sense, and multiples of the numbers 2–10.

example:
Chris Stapleton
22 + 36 = 58

• Think of the number of digits in your first name. Now double that number and add five. Write your name, the number sentences that you made to find the answer, and the total on a Post-it. Then place it on the graph where you think it belongs. (Should be intervals of 12: 1–2, 13–24, 25–36, 37–48, more than 48.)

example:
Stephanie 9 + 9 + 5 = 23
or 9 x 2 + 5 = 23

• Determine the number of letters in your first name. Determine the number of letters in your last name. Now subtract the lesser amount from the greater amount. Write your name, the number sentence, and the answer on a Post-it and place it on the graph where you think it belongs. (Should be intervals of 3: 0–3, 4–6, 7–9, more than 9.)

example:
Jessica Bamberger
9 - 7 = 2

• Think of the number of people that you live with. Multiply that number by ten. Write your name and the number that you got on a Post-it. Place it on the graph where you think it belongs. (Should be intervals of 20: 1–20, 21–40, 41–60, 61–80, more than 80.)

example:
I live with 4 other people.
4 x 10 = 40 Sarah

- Think about your telephone number (or the telephone number of the school). Subtract the smallest digit from the largest digit. Write your name, the subtraction number sentence, and your answer on a Post-it. Place it on the graph where it belongs. (Should be intervals of 3: 0–3, 4–6, 7–9.)

example:
555-7558 8 - 5 = 3

- Think about your first name. Determine the fractional part of your name that is made up of vowels. Write your name and the fraction on a Post-it. Place it on the graph where it belongs. (Should be these intervals: 0–1/2, exactly 1/2, greater than 1/2.)

example:
Paula has 3 vowels out of 5 total letters.
3/5 of the letters are vowels.

Which Is Your Favorite Season?

This lesson works nicely with a rectangle bar graph using colored strips. It also teaches the children to read a legend. If you are teaching a unit on fractions, this graph works well, too.

MATERIALS
- wipe-off marker
- rectangle graph
- colored strips of construction paper
- legend
- sentence strips

DIRECTIONS

1. Prepare a legend. Write your choices with a wipe-off marker. It may look something like this:

2. Use a different colored strip to represent each season. There should be enough strips for every child to choose each color. For example, if you have 30 children in your class, you would need 30 yellow strips, 30 green strips, 30 blue strips, and 30 orange strips.

3. Write "Which season do you like best?" on a sentence strip.

4. Place the graph in a location where all the children can see. Let children select and paste on the graph a strip that corresponds to their preference. Discuss.

The first time Patti did this graph with her children it looked something like this:

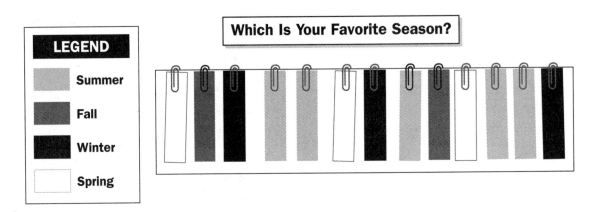

Teacher: I would like everyone to take a moment and look at our graph. (*Make sure to give the students 15–20 seconds to study the graph.*) Raise your hand if you would like to share something about the graph.

Child: The graph is in the shape of a rectangle.

Teacher: Thank you for sharing that. Who would like to share something different about what they see?

Child: I see four different colors on the graph.

Teacher: Great! Can you name the four colors?

Child: Yellow, blue, orange, and green.

Teacher: Who can tell us something different that they see?

Child: I see six blue strips.

Teacher: Would you tell us how you know that?

Child: I counted.

Teacher: Would you come up to the graph and show us how you counted?

Child: One, two, three, four, five, six blue strips. (*Child touches each one as she counts.*)

Teacher: Thank you. Can anyone else tell us something different about the graph?

Child: The strips are all mixed up.

Teacher: What do you mean by that?

Child: The colors are all mixed up. There are blue strips in between green strips and orange strips with yellow strips. It's hard to count when the strips are like this. I keep losing track of what I have counted.

Teacher: I see what you mean. The colors are all over the place. Which season do you think is the most popular? (*Ask the children to think about it and then whisper to someone nearby.*)

Child: I think winter is the most popular. I see more blue strips.

Teacher: Would anyone else like to share their opinion? (*Survey the class.*)

Child: I see more green strips, so I think it's spring.

Child: No, I think it is fall. I see more orange.

Teacher: Well, I have heard three different seasons already. I wonder how we can determine which season was the most popular? Does anyone have a strategy that will make counting the strips a little easier?

Child: We could keep a tally and record each of the colored strips.

Teacher: That's a great idea. Any others?

Child: We could sort the strips.

Teacher: What do you mean "sort the strips"?

Child: Move the strips around so all the same colors are right next to each other.

Teacher: I am not sure I know what you mean. Show us.

Child: Sure, but I am going to have to move them all around. (*Child moves the strips around. He takes all the yellows and places them next to each other and does the same with the remaining colors. When he finishes, the children tell him it looks much better and easier to read and interpret.*)

Teacher: Wow, I like that! You placed all the same colors together.

Child: I think the graph is much easier to understand. It was so mixed up before.

Teacher: Do you think this way helps us understand the information on the graph?

Child: Yes, I can see without counting that summer has the most strips.

Teacher: How do you know that?

Child: Because I see more yellow than any other color.

Teacher: That's a great strategy. I see more yellow than any other color, too.

Child: Now I can tell that winter is the least popular because I don't see a lot of blue.

Teacher: Great! Let's take a vote. (*Teacher asks children to vote on whether the graph should stay mixed up or sorted. The children say sorted.*) How can we place our strips tomorrow morning so our strips stay sorted?

Child: When we put our strips up, we should leave spaces between the colors so other people can put their strips up too.

Teacher: Sounds like a great idea. (*The other children agree.*)

The discussion can continue. You can ask them why one season is more popular than another. Patti also asked what things made each of the seasons popular. The children may say "you can build snow forts in winter and not in summer," or "you can swim in summer and not in winter."

This is how the graph looked after the colors were sorted.

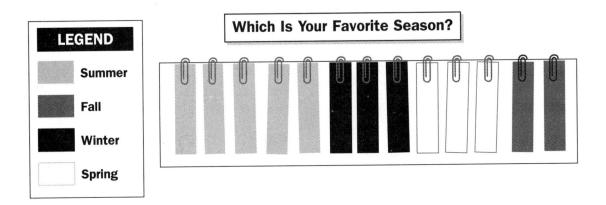

LEGEND
- Summer
- Fall
- Winter
- Spring

Which Is Your Favorite Season?

Other "Favorite" Things to Graph

The following are lists that we have compiled, by topic, of favorite things that you can graph with your students. Remember that we based these ideas on curricular areas that we and our colleagues were teaching as part of social studies, science, literature, or holidays and other special events. Use these to get you started and to spark your own ideas:

Social Studies

FOODS

type of berry: strawberry, blueberry, raspberry

kind of candy: lollipops, chocolate bar, bubble gum

breakfast food: eggs, cereal, waffles, pancakes

fruit: banana, apple, orange, grapes

ice cream: chocolate, vanilla, strawberry

sandwich: peanut butter and jelly, ham and cheese, something else

school lunch: tacos, grilled cheese, pizza

drink: milk, juice, soda, water

popsicle: fudge, grape, cherry, orange

cookie: chocolate chip, fig Newton, sugar wafer

snack food: popcorn, pretzels, potato chips, corn chip

cake: chocolate, yellow, spice

dessert: cake, ice cream, fruit, pudding

cereal: Rice Krispies, Cap'n Crunch, Kix, Cheerios

meal of the day: breakfast, lunch, dinner

soup: chicken noodle, tomato, vegetable, beef

vegetable: corn, broccoli, string beans, carrots, peas

jelly bean flavor: grape, cherry, lime, orange, lemon

way to eat an egg: scrambled, hard boiled, sunny-side up

SPECIAL DAYS

holiday: Halloween, Valentine's Day, Fourth of July, Thanksgiving

gift from the holidays: books, clothes, toys, games

day of the week: Friday, Saturday, Sunday

GETTING AROUND

kind of car: sports car, van, pick-up truck, station wagon

form of transportation: train, boat, airplane, car, bicycle, motorcycle

NEIGHBORHOOD

community worker: police officer, firefighter, construction worker, postal worker, nurse

IN AND OUT OF SCHOOL

thing to wear: sweaters, sweatshirts, shorts, jeans

thing to write with: pencil, pen, marker, crayon

special at school: art, music, p.e., library, computer lab

thing to do after school: homework, relax, watch T.V., exercise, play sports, read

subject at school: reading, science, math, social studies, writing

ANIMALS

animal: tiger, bear, horse, dog, cat

JUST FOR FUN

story character: Corduroy, Doctor DeSoto, Berenstain Bears

cartoon character: Snoopy, Mickey Mouse, Donald Duck, Casper

place to swim: ocean, lake, swimming pool

favorite book: provide three choices

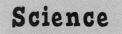

Science

WEATHER/SEASONS/TIME

kind of weather: sunny, cloudy, rainy, stormy

color: blue, purple, green, red, yellow

time of day: morning, afternoon, evening

summer activity: swimming, camping, hiking, bicycling, jogging

winter activity: sledding, skiing, skating

season: fall, winter, spring, summer

OTHER

kind of toothpaste: Aim, Crest, Colgate

superhero: whatever is popular at the time

movie: whatever is popular at the time

sports team: choose local area teams

T.V. show: choose from what is popular at the time

Which of These Jobs Do You Think Is the Most Important?

In this lesson, the teacher provided each child with pictures of a doctor, a teacher, and a parent. Children were told to select the picture of the job that they thought was the most important, and place it on the graph. Then it was time to analyze the data.

MATERIALS
- pictures of doctor, teacher, parent
- paste or glue

TEACHER/STUDENT EXCHANGE

Teacher: Look at the graph. What do you see?

Child: I see lots of pictures.

Child: Our graph has not had pictures before.

Child: This was the first time that we had to color our choices.

Child: The doctor was the most important.

Teacher: How did you know that?

Child: It's the longest one.

Child: It also has the most.

Child: None of the others are as long as it is.

Teacher: Think of some reasons why you think people thought that the doctor had the most important job. (*Give children their ten seconds of "think" time. Then let them "pair" with a friend to talk about what they were thinking.*) Who would like to share something that you heard or something that you were thinking?

Child: Doctors take care of people, so that's why people thought they were the most important.

Child: They take care of sick people and make them better.

Teacher: What about parents? They take care of us when we are sick, don't they?

Child: Yeah, but doctors go to school for a long time to learn how to take care of people. Parents don't.

Child: Only doctors can give out medicine and operate on you when you feel bad. Parents can't do that.

Child: Doctors are also paid a lot to do their job.

Teacher: So, you think that that makes them more important?

Child: Well, it's important to make money, but parents and doctors are both important.

Child: It was really hard to choose.

Child: Parents take care of you every day of your life and doctors don't.

Child: Teachers are important because without them all of the children in the world would never learn about any of this stuff.

Teacher: So, what you're saying is that all of these jobs are important and it was very difficult to decide which was the most important one.

This discussion continued. It was clear that they understood the different responsibilities of the three jobs and were convinced that all three were important. This was a wonderful way to begin the Social Studies unit on occupations.

Let's Measure Our Feet

In today's world, measurement plays a key role in everyday life. Carpenters measure when building a new home. Tailors take measurements of our waist and arm length to design clothing that fits us properly. Our cars are equipped with speedometers to help us monitor our speed. In the kitchen we are constantly aware of measurements through our use of measuring spoons and cups. As adults it is necessary to perform measuring tasks efficiently. However, children enjoy exploring the how longs? and how many? of their own world. They develop useful strategies when comparing and contrasting information they have collected.

MATERIALS
- unifix cubes/connecting cubes
- paper
- pencil
- scissors
- bar graph

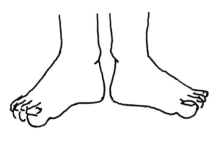

DIRECTIONS

Have each child trace his/her foot onto paper. Cut out the shape. Make sure children have cubes in reach to do this activity.

Teacher: Today we are going to use the feet we have cut out to collect data about ourselves. Take a look at your foot. If you would like to share something about your foot, raise your hand.

Child: I have a big foot.

Teacher: Thank you. Would anyone else like to share? (*Teacher calls on several students.*)

Child: My foot is longer than Paul's.

Teacher: Great! How do you know that?

Child: It just looks longer.

Child: My foot is not as wide as his foot.

Child: We traced our feet in different colors.

Child: My foot is much shorter than his.

Teacher: Wow, we certainly have a lot to say about our feet. Right now I'd like you to take a look at the cubes that are on our tables. Without picking the cubes up, I'd like you to think about this. I would like you to make a prediction. Do you think you could fit more cubes on the inside of your foot or around the outside of your foot? Or do you think the number will be the same? (*Give children time to think about this.*)

Child: I think that I will be able to fit more cubes on the inside of my foot than on the outside.

Teacher: You do? Why do you think that?

Child: Well, my foot looks very wide.

Teacher: I see. Would anyone else like to share their prediction?

Child: I think I will be able to use more cubes around the outside of my foot.

Teacher: Why do you feel that way?

Child: Because every time I go to get new shoes, my mom always complains that the bigger my foot gets, the more money the shoe costs.

Teacher: It seems like children's feet are always growing!

At this time allow the children to use the cubes and actually test their predictions. Then bring the class back together to continue the discussion.

Teacher: What have your discovered about your own foot?

Child: I can fit 14 cubes on the inside, and 12 cubes on the outside.

Teacher: What does that tell you about your foot?

Child: The inside of my foot is a little bigger than the outside.

Teacher: Good! How about someone else?

Child: I can fit the same number of cubes on the inside as around the outside.

Teacher: What does that tell you about your foot?

Child: The inside of my foot is as big as the outside.

Continue the discussion for a few moments longer. Ask the children to check out their predictions as well. When working with older children this is an excellent way to introduce area and perimeter. *How Big is a Foot?* by Rolf Myller, works well with these topics.

Teacher: I'd like to make a graph of all this information. How can we show the data we collected?

Child: We could graph our predictions.

Teacher: What should we include?

Teacher elicits the original predictions and records on paper: The inside of my foot has more cubes than the outside, the inside of my foot has the same number of cubes as the outside, the inside of my foot has fewer cubes than the outside of my foot. Guide the children into placing their original predictions properly on the graph. Allow some time to discuss the class findings about their feet.

Money From Home

OVERVIEW

All children use money. We've found that while children like to sort coins, count coins, and even collect coins, there remains a lot of confusion about how to use the fewest number of coins to show amounts. Young children also have great difficulty making change.

We use paper coins to show the number of days the children have been in school. We ask children to show this amount in as many ways as possible, and with the fewest coins possible. Students are encouraged to look for ways to exchange coins without changing the value of the amount shown.

By collecting data with coins, we've found that children get to practice counting, comparing, and using coins. Our students have greater facility with coins as a result.

MATERIALS

- pencil and paper
- coins from parent
- large sheet of bulletin board paper
- markers
- small squares of construction paper, assorted colors
- scissors

DIRECTIONS

1. Ask children to prepare for the next day's lesson by doing some data collecting at home. Tell them to ask Mom for all the coins in her purse/wallet, or ask Dad for all the change in his pocket. Ask children to record the number of pennies, nickels, dimes, quarters, and half-dollars they find. Remind the children to bring this information (not the coins!) in the next day.

2. Explain to the students that they are going to create a graph to represent the information they collected from home.

TEACHER/STUDENT EXCHANGE

Teacher: Today we are going to share the information that we collected last night. I'd like for you to take a minute and turn to someone nearby and share your results. Now raise your hand if you'd like to share your results.

Child: I had 6 quarters, 5 dimes, 7 nickels, and 14 pennies.

Teacher: Thank you for sharing that with us. Who else would like to share results with the class?

Child: My mom had 2 quarters, 8 dimes, 3 nickels and 3 pennies.

Teacher: Thank you. I noticed that neither of you had half-dollars. I wonder why?

Child: I don't think there are as many half-dollars in circulation as the other coins. They're not as popular.

Teacher: I think you're right. Any other reasons why we don't see many half-dollars?

Child: My mom thinks they are too big and heavy and she doesn't like to carry them.

Teacher: I agree, they are kind of big. Any other ideas?

Child: I know a lot of people who collect them.

Teacher: You're right. Does anyone else know people who collect coins? (*Several children raise their hands.*)

Child: Coin collecting is very popular.

Teacher: Let's continue sharing our results. (*Several other children share, then teacher thinks aloud.*) I wonder how we can show our results on a graph.

Child: We could cut out different colored coin shapes to represent what we collected.

Teacher: That's a great idea! What else could we do?

Child: We could write the coin's name and then place tally marks after each one.

Teacher: Boys and girls, you have some great ideas. I can tell you are thinking.

Child: I think they are all good ideas, but I think we will have too many coins to show. We may run out of room.

Teacher: What gave you that idea?

Child: Well, my partner and I have 33 coins between the two of us. We have 26 children in this class. That's a lot of coins.

Teacher: You're right. I didn't think about that. What could we do?

Child: I think if we were to cut out lots of circles that would take up a lot of time, and besides, we don't have any silver- or copper-colored paper.

Teacher: That's a good point. What else could we use so we can see and represent the data we collected?

Child: I know! Let's just cut out squares. They're easy and won't take a lot of time.

Teacher: Great. But how will we know which square is for which coin?

Child: We will just use a different color for each coin. And so we don't have to cut so many squares we'll say that each square stands for 2 coins.

Teacher: That sounds like a super idea. How will we know which coin stands for which color?

Child: Make a legend. I'll do that.

Teacher: Where will we put all this information?

Child: We'll need a great big piece of paper.

Teacher: Let's choose colors so we can get started. (*Teacher distributes colored construction paper to groups and instructs the children to cut squares to represent what they collected. Give them a few minutes to work and then have them join you in a large area on the floor.*)

Teacher: Now that we have our squares to represent our data, let's decide how to set up the graph. (*She takes several responses and they decide as a class how to display.*)

Child: I think we should set it up horizontally and just glue our squares in rows.

Teacher: Sounds great. Show us what you mean by "in rows." (*Child lays squares in rows and sorts the colors as she does so.*)

Child: I like what _____ has done, but I would like the coins to be in order according to their value. Pennies first because they are worth the least.

Teacher: How do the rest of you feel about that? (*Children agree that it makes sense.*) Who would like to place their squares down next?

Child: I would like to go next. (*Child places squares down but stops when he gets to the quarter.*)

Teacher: You look like you're thinking. What are you thinking about?

Child: Well, I have 7 quarters and each square = 2 coins. I put 3 down so far which means 6, and now I'm not sure what to do because I have 7 quarters.

Teacher: Hmmm, I see what you mean. What could we do?

Child: I know! Let's cut a square in half.

Teacher: Why do you want to cut the square in half?

Child: Because if a whole square equals 2, then half of a square should equal 1.

Teacher: How do the rest of you feel about that? (*Children agree upon the strategy.*) Let's continue to lay our squares out on the paper. (*When the children have completed this task, the teacher continues.*)

Teacher: I think it looks great. Whenever I see a square I know that means two. I wonder how we can let others know one square means two.

Child: We'll need to make a key. 1 square = 2 coins.

Teacher: Well, now that we've got it all set up, let's take a look together at the information.

Teacher and children engage in a discussion. Again she begins the discussion simply by saying, "Who can tell us something about the graph?" Children may say anything that they notice about the coins, which coin had the most, which had the least, why some had more than others, and so forth.

Estimating Scoops of Rice

Our Viewpoint

In lessons on estimation, as well as other areas, such as predicting and computing, we suggest that you spend a great deal of time talking with your students about their work. Talk with them about the strategies they use to get answers and ask many students to express how they arrived at their conclusions.

For example, if you ask students to estimate an answer, also ask them to explain their reasoning. Children have surprised us with some unique and very "sensible" ways to arrive at answers to problems. They need to be given opportunities to share these ways so that others can learn. There is not just one right way to solve a problem.

MATERIALS
- marker
- index cards
- three 2-liter clear, plastic bottles (empty)
- rice
- scoops and funnels for pouring
- sealed, clear, plastic 2-liter bottle filled with rice

DIRECTIONS

As you can see, this is a bottle graph. (See pages 30–31 for further information.)

Children are to predict the number of scoops of rice that are in the sealed container. They "cast their vote" by putting a scoop of rice into the liter bottle that represents their choice. Then the discussion begins.

Teacher: Boys and girls, look at the three bottles. What can you say about what you see? (*Give them ten seconds.*) Whisper to a friend what you were just thinking about. (*Give them time to talk.*) Who would like to say something that they heard or something that they were thinking about?

Child: It's different looking at bottles than looking at a paper graph.

Teacher: Tell us what you mean by "different."

Child: When we have paper you can tell how many people put their names up, but with the bottles, you can't tell how many scoops. Also, you can't tell who put their scoop into which bottle.

Teacher: So, this is a different kind of graph than the kind that we usually make. Who would like to say something else?

Child: The highest bottle was the one that said "9–16."

Teacher: What does that tell us about what people in the class were thinking?

Child: Most people thought that there were between 9 and 16 scoops of rice in the big container.

Teacher: How did you know that?

Child: See, the more scoops that people put into the bottles the higher the rice inside got. So, if that one was the highest that means that more people thought that there were between 9 and 16 scoops in the big container.

Child: I thought there were 12, so I put my rice scoop in that bottle.

Child: I thought there were 15.

Child: So did I.

Teacher: Would someone talk about how you decided how many scoops there might be in the big container?

Child: I put the scoop at the end of the container and measured how many scoops long the container was. It was 4 scoops long. It was 2 scoops high and it was 2 scoops wide. So, I thought the bottom was going to have 8 full scoops and there would be two layers of scoops. So, I put my scoop of rice in the 9–16 because I figured it would be 16 scoops full.

Child: I did it a different way, but I put my scoop of rice in the same bottle. At first I thought that it might be twenty. But I kind of looked at it and thought that twenty was too much. Ten seemed too little, so I just picked 15 since that was in between.

Teacher: Would someone who picked a different bottle talk about why they chose that range?

Child: There's a lot of scoops in that container. It's pretty big. So, I thought that it had to be in the bottle that had the most scoops. It couldn't be less than 16. That's not enough.

Teacher: Let's talk about this for about five more minutes. Then let's talk about how to find out exactly how many scoops there are in the big container.

More Graphing Ideas Across the Curriculum

The following ideas are those we selected based on social studies and science units that are often taught in grade one through grade four. We've categorized them to make it easier for you to use them as part of a unit that you may teach.

Social Studies

COLORS

- Look at your clothing today. What color are you wearing the most of? White, blue, black, red, some other color.

- What color car do you think that there are the most of on the road? Red, black, white, green, blue, some other color.

- What color is your best friend's hair? Black, brown, red, blond.

- What is your favorite color in the rainbow? Red, orange, yellow, green, blue, indigo, violet.

- Pretend that you are sad. What color would make you happy? Red, blue, yellow, orange, green, some other color.

- What color is your favorite fruit? Orange, red, yellow, green, some other color.

- Think of the paint colors yellow, red, and blue. If you mixed two colors, what color would you make? Orange, green, purple.

- What color do you think is the most exciting? Yellow, orange, red, green, blue, purple, some other color.

COMMUNITY WORKERS

- Which community worker do you think has the most dangerous job? A firefighter, a construction worker, a police officer.

- Which job do you think is the messiest? An auto mechanic, a garbage collector, a doctor, a farmer.

- Which job do you think would be the most fun? The president, a dentist, a store clerk, a chef.

CONTINENTS

A clothespin graph (with yes/no categories) might be good for the following:

- After discussing a country/continent ask:

  - Have you ever visited this country/continent?

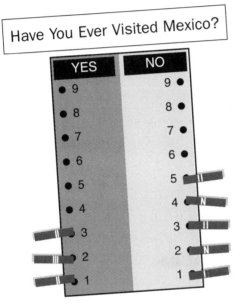

- Would you like to visit this country/continent?

- Do you know anyone who was born in this country/continent?

- Do you know anyone who speaks a language from this country/continent?

- Have you read any books about this country/continent?

- Have you tasted food that comes from this country/continent?

- Have you ever seen the clothing from this country/continent?

- Do you know anyone who has money from this country/continent?

- If you have many children who speak languages other than English, create a graph to show what other languages they know. For example, the title could be "Languages That I Speak."

- If you have a class that is fairly culturally diverse, you can survey the children to find out which country they were born in (or which country their parents were born in). Then a graph of either continents, countries, or regions of the world can be created.

TRANSPORTATION

- I'd rather come to school on/in: a motorcycle, a hot air balloon, a helicopter, a sailboat.

- Which ground vehicle would you like to learn how to operate? Tractor-trailer truck, bus, van, car, motorcycle.

- Which form of transportation do you think is the fastest? Airplane, train, motorcycle, speedboat.

THE FARM

- On a farm, which animal would a farmer have the most of? Chickens, horses, cows, pigs, sheep.

- Which four-legged farm animal would you like to be? Horse, cow, pig, goat, sheep.

- On a farm which animal do you think is the most important? Horses, chickens, cows, pigs.

- Which fruit trees do you think farmers have more of? Apples, peaches, pears, oranges.

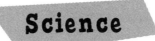

Science

ANIMALS

- Which animal do you think is the friendliest? Lion, tiger, bear, walrus.

- Which animal would you rather be? Giraffe, cow, horse, monkey.

- Which animal do you think is the funniest? Elephant, gorilla, hyena, squirrel.

- Which animal do you think is the cutest? Penguin, monkey, zebra.

- Which would you rather have as a pet? Dog, horse, cat, bird, fish.

DINOSAURS

- If you were a dinosaur, which one would you rather be? Apatosaurus, triceratops, pterodactyl, stegosaurus.

- Which dinosaur do you think is the most dangerous? Stegosaurus, pterodactyl, velociraptor, tyrannosaurus rex.

- Which dinosaur would you like to have as a pet? Apatosaurus, triceratops, anklyosaurus, coelophyphus.

- Which dinosaur do you think is the prettiest? Velociraptor, apatosaurus, triceratops, tyrannosaurus rex.

ELECTRICITY

- The total number of light switches in my home is: 0–2, 3–5, 6–8, more than 8.

- The number of things that run on electricity that I can name is: 0–3, 4–6, 7–9, more than 9.

- My home is heated by: electricity, gas heat, solar energy, wood-burning stove, fireplace, some other form of heat.

THE ENVIRONMENT

- Which thing that people do to the environment makes you the most angry? Littering, chopping down a tree, killing an animal for its fur, something else.

- What's the easiest thing you can do to make our Earth a nicer place? Recycle, pick up trash, conserve energy.

- Which do you think would be more important to do to save the environment? Save the rainforest, save an animal on the endangered species list, save the rivers.

- Where would you rather live? In the mountains, in a big city, near the ocean.

MAGNETS

- How many nails will your magnet pick up? 0–5, 6–10, more than 10.

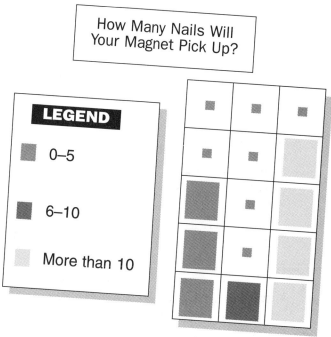

How Many Nails Will Your Magnet Pick Up?

LEGEND

■ 0–5

■ 6–10

■ More than 10

- Which of these magnets do you think is the strongest? Horseshoe, bar, refrigerator.

- Which do you think your magnet will not pick up? Aluminum foil, screw, nail, screwdriver, piece of wood.

OCEAN LIFE

- Which invertebrate do you think is the most interesting to learn about? Crab, sea anemone, scallop, squid, jellyfish.

- Which marine mammal do you think is the most friendly to humans? Whale, dolphin, seal, sea otter, manatee.

- If you were a sea dweller, which would you rather be? Barracuda, seastar, octopus, moray eel, shark.

- Which tidal pool creature do you know the most about? Hermit crab, sea urchin, sea anemone, barnacle.

- Which animal lives closest to the ocean floor? Eel, octopus, humpback whale, dolphin.

PLANTS AND SEEDS

- Give the children a cup of seeds (Explain that dried beans are seeds.) Have them sort them. Graph how you sorted these: by color, by size, by shape

- What type of seed do you have the most of?

- What type of seed do you have the least of?

- More of your seeds are: flat, round, fat, oval.

- What color are most of your seeds? White, brown, tan, gray, some other color.

- What do you think your plant needs the most of? Sunshine, water, light, something else.

- How many centimeters tall is your plant? (Depending on the type of plant it is, give a range: 0–4 cm, 5–8 cm, more than 8 cm.)

- Which kind of bean will sprout first? Kidney bean, pinto bean, lima bean, other.)

- Where do you think a plant will live the longest? In the closet, on the porch, by the window.

- Look at your plant. How many leaves are on your plant? (Depending on the type of plant it is, give a range: 0–3, 4–7, more than 7.)

SINK OR FLOAT?

- Choose one thing that you think will float in water: marble, bar of soap, Ping Pong ball, rock.

- Choose one thing that you think will sink in water: coin, cork, rock, paper.

- Choose one thing that you think will float in oil: cork, paper, bar of soap, Ping Pong ball.

- Choose one thing that you think will sink in oil: pencil, marker, crayon, eraser.

WEATHER

- On a snowy day, which would you rather wear to keep you warm? Hat, mittens, boots, scarf, gloves.

- Think about the month that is coming up. Which kind of weather will we have the most of: rainy, snowy, cloudy, windy, sunny?

- How many days during the month of _____ do you think will be sunny? Between 0–10, between 10–20, between 20–31.

- How many days during the month of _____ do you think will be rainy? Between 0–10, between 10–20, between 20–31.

- How many inches of snow do you predict we will have this winter? 0–2 inches, 3–5 inches, more than 5 inches of snow. (If it's more appropriate, do this for rainfall.)

- What do you predict will be the coldest temperature this month? (Give a range according to the season.)

- What do you predict will be the warmest temperature this month? (Give a range according to the season.)

- What will today's temperature be at 12:00 p.m.? (Give a range according to the season.)

- As a longer project, students could create a line graph to record the temperature, in Farenheit or Celsius, for an entire month. Have students discuss rises and falls in the temperature. Have them talk about the range in temperatures, the difference between the highest and lowest temperature, and the average temperature during the month. Have them predict what the next month's graph will look like based on the data collected from this month. Have them write about this predicted graph and explain why they made their predictions.

AREA/PERIMETER/ LENGTH OR CIRCUMFERENCE

• Count how many footsteps it is from your desk to the classroom door: 0–5, 6–10, 11–15, 16–20, more than 20. (vertical or horizontal bar graph, circle or rectangle graph)

• Take out a pencil from your desk. Use centimeter cubes to determine the length of this pencil. Write this length on a Post-it along with your name and put it on the graph where it belongs. What is the length of your pencil? 0–5 centimeters, 6–10 centimeters, 11–15 centimeters, more than 20 centimeters. (vertical or horizontal bar graph, circle or rectangle graph)

• Use connecting links to determine the circumference of your head and the circumference of your waist. Determine the difference between these two measures and write this on a Post-it along with your name. Put the Post-it on the graph where it belongs. What is the difference? Less than 5, 5–10, 10–15, greater than 15. (vertical or horizontal bar graph, quadrant graph, circle or rectangle graph)

• Put your foot on a piece of paper and trace around it. Use connecting links and lay these on top of your outlined foot. How many connecting links does it take to go around your foot? Between 0–10, between 11–20, more than 20. (vertical or horizontal bar graph; for a string graph, use the connected links and hang them up so they can be compared with the other connected links.)

TIME

- What time did you get up this morning? Before 7:00 a.m., 7:00–7:30 a.m., 7:30–8:00 a.m., 8:00–8:30 a.m., after 8:30 a.m. (vertical or horizontal bar graph, rectangle or circle graph)

- How much time do you think it would take you to walk a mile? About 10 minutes, about 15 minutes, about 20 minutes, more than 20 minutes. (vertical or horizontal bar graph, rectangle or circle graph)

- How many hours of sleep do you usually get each night? More than 8, less than 8. (clothespin graph—yes/no type, vertical or horizontal bar graph, circle or rectangle graph)

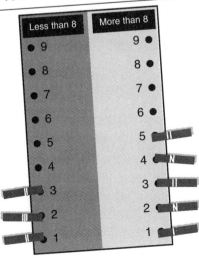

How Many Hours of Sleep Do You Usually Get Each Night?

- How much time do you spend on homework each night? About 15 minutes, 15 minutes–half hour, half hour–45 minutes, 45 minutes–one hour, more than one hour. (vertical or horizontal bar graph, circle or rectangle graph)

- What time is your favorite television program on? Just before school, just after school, but before dinner, right after dinner, before my bath or shower, after my bath or shower. (vertical or horizontal bar graph, circle or rectangle graph)

MONEY

Modify these ideas to best meet the needs of your students. If the activity calls for using quarters and your students haven't been exposed to them yet, don't use them.

- Coin Toss: Take two pennies from the bowl of pennies at your table. Flip both of these coins once. Show the result of your toss by putting your name on a Post-it and placing it on the graph where it belongs: 2 heads, 2 tails, 1 head and 1 tail. (vertical and horizontal bar graph, rectangle graph or circle graph)

- Which coin do you think weighs more? A penny, a nickel, or a dime? Take a replica of this coin and put it where you think it belongs. (vertical or horizontal bar graph)

- Close your eyes and pick 3 coins from the bowl (the bowl has pennies and nickels only). Choose the place on the graph that shows what you picked: all pennies, all nickels, more pennies than nickels, more nickels than pennies. (quadrant graph, vertical or horizontal bar graph)

- Which coin do you like best? Penny, nickel, dime. Take a paper replica of this coin and put it on the graph where it belongs. (vertical or horizontal bar graph) If older students do this activity, it would be worthwhile to have them write about why they chose the coin that they did.

- How much do you have? Close your eyes and take a handful of pennies and nickels. Determine the value of these coins. Write this value on a Post-it along with your name. Put this on the graph where you think it belongs. 1–25 cents, 26–50 cents, 51–75 cents, more than 75 cents (vertical or horizontal bar or rectangle or quadrant graph)

- How many pennies? Close your eyes and take a handful of pennies. How many did you take? Put the total and your name on a Post-it and place it on the graph where you think it belongs: Less than 10, 10–20, more than 20. (vertical or horizontal bar graph, rectangle or circle graph)

- Pick an amount of money from 1 to 25 cents. Now double this amount and add a nickel. Write the number sentences to show your work and write the total, along with your name, on a Post-it and place it on the graph where it belongs: 1–15 cents, 16–30 cents, 31–45 cents, more than 45 cents. (vertical or horizontal bar graph)

- Penny Flip: Take a penny from the bowl of pennies at your table. Flip this penny and use the graph to show whether you flipped "heads" or "tails." Heads/Tails graph. (Clothespin graphs are good for this.)

Prediction, Estimation, Computation

Use the following ideas to help your students develop their skills in prediction, estimation, and computation. We've organized them by suggested grade levels.

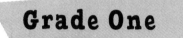

Grade One

- Which holiday do you think the most people like best? Halloween, Thanksgiving, Valentine's Day.

- Do you predict that there are more boys or more girls in the first grade today?

- Which football/baseball/basketball team do you think will win the game on Sunday?

- Which flavor juice do you think the most people in our class like the best? Grape juice, Hawaiian Punch, orange juice, apple juice.

- (Put multilink or Unifix cubes inside a small cardboard box. Children may shake the box, but they should not be able to see inside.) How many multilink cubes are in the box? 10–20, 20–30, 30–40, more than 40.

- Put pretzel sticks inside a transparent jar. How many pretzel sticks are in the jar? More than 25, less than 25.

- Put cotton balls inside a transparent jar. How many cotton balls are inside the jar? More than 25, less than 25.

- How many shoes are there in our classroom today? More than 25, less than 25.

- My age is: More than 6, less than 6, exactly 6.

- If we counted all of the fingers in our classroom today, how many would there be? More than 100, 100–200, more than 200.

- If we add 1 to the number of people who live in our house, the number would be: 2–4, 4–6, more than 6.

- If we take 1 away from the number of people who live in our house the number would be: 1–3, 3–5, exactly 5, more than 5.

- This graph is to be done during an election year. Who do you predict will be the next president/governor/mayor?

- This is a good graph to do on a day that the teacher is absent. Where do you think your teacher is today? At home sick, at a meeting, out of town, some other place.

- What do you predict the weather will be like this afternoon at 3:30 p.m.? Cloudy, rainy, sunny, windy, snowy.

- Look at the number of buttons on your clothes. For each button take one cube. Look at the number of pockets on your clothes. For each pocket take two cubes. Put the two groups of cubes together. Write this total and your name on a Post-it and put it on the graph where it belongs: 0–7, 8–14, 14–21, more than 21.

- Think about getting all of your spelling words right on the test. Predict what your family might say. "That's terrific!" "You did great!" "How'd you do that?" Something else.

- Think about taking a fact test with 20 addition facts. Predict how many you will get correct. All of them, 17–20, 14–17, less than 14.

- Predict how many times you can clap your hands in half a minute. Less than 20 times, exactly 20 times, more than 20 times.

- The date of my birthday is a: Single-digit number, double-digit number.

- Predict how many times you can jump in a minute. More than 30 jumps, less than 30 jumps, exactly 30 jumps.

- Suppose that A=1, B=2, C=1, D=2, E=1, F=2, G=1 . . . Z. Figure out what your name is worth. Write your name, the addition number sentence, and the total on a Post-it. Put it on the graph where you think it belongs: 0–8, 9–16, more than 16.

- Predict what number you can count up to in one minute. Up to 50, up to 100, up to 150, more than 150.

For the next five graphs, a two-column graph would work nicely.

• Write your first name on a Post-it. Write the number of letters that you have in your name. Do you have an "even" or an "odd" number of letters?

• Write your first and last name on a Post-it. Write the number of letters that you have in both your names combined. Do you have an "even" or an "odd" number of letters?

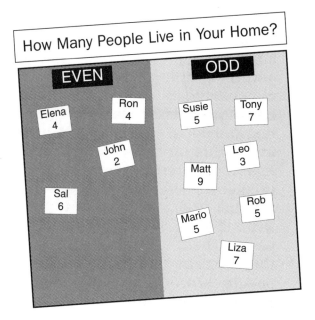

• Think of your telephone number. Write your name and the last digit of your telephone number on a Post-it. Is the last digit of your number "even" or "odd"?

• Think of the number of people who live in your home. Write this number on a Post-it along with your name. Is the total number of people "even" or "odd"?

• Think of a "doubles fact." Write your name and the fact on a Post-it note. Put it on the graph to show where the answer would be: 0–8, 9–16, 17–24.

• Think of the date of your birthday. Does the date have a zero in the ten's place, a one in the ten's place, a two in the ten's place, or a three in the ten's place? Put your name and the date on a Post-it note and put it on the graph where it belongs.

• Put your hand on a piece of paper and trace around it. Fill the inside of the drawing with cubes. Figure out how many cubes you have used. Write your name and the number of cubes on a Post-it note and put it on the graph where it belongs: 5–10, 11–15, 15–20, more than 20.

• Stretch your hand out onto a piece of paper. Put a dot to show where your "pinkie" would be. Put a dot to show where your thumb would be. Draw a line connecting these dots. Put cubes on top of this line. Write your name on a Post-it note and the number of cubes you used. Put the Post-it note on the graph where it belongs: 1–4, 5–8, more than 8.

• Use a "predicting jar" every week. Fill it with different objects, some of which can be related to the time of year (i.e., candy corns for Halloween, different nuts for Thanksgiving, cotton balls for snow, candy hearts for Valentine's Day, etc.). Have children write their predictions on paper. Then at the end of the week, sort the papers into groups. These groups could be: 0–50, 51–100, 101–150, 51–200, more than 200. Put these papers onto a graph and discuss the results. Then come up with a way to count the objects. Try different ways each time (counting by twos, fives, tens, twenties, ones).

• Instead of counting items, a jar can be filled with sand, water, rice, beans, or other small objects, and the graphing activity could be: "How many scoops are in this jar?" Again, children predict the number and write it on paper. Then they sort the papers into groups. These can then be graphed and the graph discussed.

• Predict how much snowfall/rainfall we will get during the next three months. The range will differ based on whether it's snow or rain, and also which part of the country you live in. For example: 0–3 inches, 4–6 inches, 6–9 inches, more than 9 inches.

• Think about the number of children in our class. Predict whether less than half will buy lunch today, more than half will buy lunch today, exactly half will buy lunch today.

• Think about the number of children in our class. Predict how many total cavities there are altogether: 0–2, 3–4, 4–6, more than 6

• Flip a bicolored chip (commercially made red/yellow chip) ten times and keep a record of how many times each color lands face up. Then predict what color will be face up on the next (11th) flip. Write your name and the color on a Post-it note and put it on the graph where it belongs.

• Think about the month that we are now in. Predict how many sunny days we will have this month: 0–5, 6–10, 11–15, 16–20, more than 20.

• Choose one of your spelling words that has more than 5 letters. Is the number of vowels less than half of the word, exactly half of the word, more than half of the word?

- Choose one of your spelling words that has more than 5 letters. Is there an even or an odd number of letters?

- Choose the spelling word that has the most letters. Is the first letter in the first half of the alphabet or in the second half of the alphabet?

- Choose the spelling word that has the fewest number of letters. Is the last letter a vowel or a consonant?

- Suppose that A=1, B=2, C=3, D=1, E=2, F=3, G=1, . . . Z. Figure out the total number of points for your first name. Write the number sentence, the total, and your name on a Post-it and put it on the graph where it belongs: 0–8, 9–16, 17–24, more than 24.

- Suppose that A=5, B=10, C=5, D=10, E=5, F=10, . . . Z. Figure out the total number of points for your first name. Write the number sentence, the total, and your name on a Post-it and put it on the graph where it belongs: 0–20, 21–40, 41–60, more than 60.

- Think of the last two digits from your telephone number. Write this two-digit number and your name on a Post-it. Place it on the graph where it belongs: 0–30, 31–60, 61–90, more than 90.

- Think of the numbers 0–9. Pick a number and double it. Write your name and the number sentence on a Post-it and put it on the graph where it belongs: 0–6, 7–12, 13–18.

- Think of your telephone number. Subtract the smallest number from the largest number. Write your name and this subtraction number sentence on a Post-it and put it on the graph to show the answer: 0–3, 4–6, 7–9.

- Think of a double-digit number between 10 and 50. Write that number on a Post-it note. Reverse the digits and add that double-digit number to the original number. Write your name on this same Post-it. Put this on the graph where it belongs: 0–50, 51–100, 101–150.

- Think about the number of children in our class. Predict how many total teeth have been lost by everyone altogether: 0–4, 5–8, more than 8.

- Think of an odd number between 0 and 10. Write that number on a Post-it note and add 5 to it. Show this addition number sentence and write your name on the same Post-it. Put this on the graph where it belongs: 0–8, 9–10, 11–15.

- Think of a three-digit number between 100 and 500. Write your name and that number on a Post-it. Add the three digits together and write the number sentence that you make. Put this on the graph where it belongs: 0–7, 8–14, 15–21, more than 21.

- Think of a two-digit number that is less than 99 but more than 25. Write this number and your name on a Post-it. Is the digit in the ten's place: 0–3, 4–6, 7–9? Put your Post-it on the graph where it belongs.

Grades Three and Four

- Do this predicting graph after the children have been in school for at least 50 days. Predict when the hundredth day of school will be: before January 15th, between January 15th and February 1st, between February 1st and February 15th, between February 15th and March 1st, after March 1st.

- Predict the number of footsteps it would take to walk from the classroom to the principal's office. Write the amount and your name on a Post-it and put it on the graph where it belongs: 0–30, 31–60, 61–90, more than 90

- Predict how many children it would take to form a "ring" around the entire school. Write your name and prediction on a Post-it and put it on the graph where it belongs: less than 200, 201–400, 401–600, more than 600

- Think of the calendar and that January 1st is the first day of the year. Figure out on which day of the year your birthday falls. Write this number, your name, and the date of your birthday on a Post-it note and put it on the graph where it belongs: 1st–100th, 101st–200th, 201st–300th, 301st–365/366th.

- Estimate the number of gallons of water that a bathtub holds. Write this number and your name on a Post-it note and put it on the graph where it belongs: 0–15, 16–30, 31–45, 46–60, more than 60.

- Suppose that A=1, B=10, C=100, D=1, E=10, F=100, G=1, . . . Z. Figure out the value of your first name. Write the number sentence, the answer, and your name on a Post-it note. Put it on the graph where it belongs: 0–75, 76–150, 151–225, 226–300, more than 300.

- Predict how many times you can write your name, in cursive script, in one minute. Write your name and your prediction on a Post-it and put it on the graph where it belongs: less than 10, 10–20, 21–30, 31–40, 41–50, more than 50.

- Think of the alphabet and assign the value of 1 to A, 2 to B, 3 to C, 4 to D, 5 to E, 6 to F, . . . 26 to Z. Figure out the value of your first name and write the number sentence, the answer, and your name on a Post-it and put it on the graph where it belongs: 0–30, 31–60, 61–90, 90–120, more than 120.

- Think of your telephone number. Write a number sentence on a Post-it that shows the sum of the last four digits. Write your name and put this on the graph where it belongs: 0–10, 11–20, 21–30, 31–40.

- Think of the first three digits of your telephone number. Write these on a Post-it. Think of the last three digits of your telephone number. Write these on the same Post-it and add these two three-digit numbers together. Write your name and the sum and put the Post-it on the graph where it belongs: less than 250, 250-500, 501-750, 751-1000, more than 1000.

- Think of the first three digits of your telephone number. Write these on a Post-it. Think of the last three digits of your telephone number. Write these on the same Post-it. Set up a subtraction number sentence and subtract the smaller three-digit number from the larger three-digit number. Put a "loop" around the answer, write your name, and put the Post-it on the graph where it belongs: 0-250, 251-500, 501-750, 751-999.

• Write down the seven digits of your telephone number as if it were a seven-digit number. Look at the digit in the thousand's place (you can also point out any other place). Is this digit: 0–3, 4–6, 7–9?

• Think of a three-digit number. Write this number and your name on a Post-it. Double this number and write the number sentence that you form. Put the Post-it on the graph where it belongs: 200–500, 501–800, 801–1100, 1101–1400, 1401–1700, 1701–2000.

• Think of an even number between 0 and 20. Count the number of letters in your first name and add it to this number. Write the number sentence that you have created and put this and your name on a Post-it and place it on the graph where it belongs: 0–5, 6–10, 11–15, 16–20, 20–25, more than 25.

• Look at the clothing that you are wearing. Suppose that each button on your clothing is worth a dime and each pocket is worth a nickel. Determine how much money you would get for the clothing that you are wearing. Write this amount on a Post-it along with your name. Place this on a graph where you think it belongs: 0 cents–25 cents, 26 cents–50 cents, 51 cents–75 cents, 76 cents–$1.00, more than $1.00.

• Think of an odd number between 10 and 50. Subtract 10 from this number and write the subtraction number sentence that you have created on a Post-it. Circle the answer and write your name. Place this on the graph where you think it belongs: 0–20, 21–40, more than 40.

• Think of the number that represents the month that you were born. Double that number. Then put your name and that doubled number on a Post-it note and put it on the graph where it belongs. 0–4, 5–8, 9–12, 13–16, 17–20, more than 20. Encourage students to consider why no odd numbers appear on the Post-its.

• Take your age and multiply it by 3. Using the number that you get, subtract the number that is the last digit of your telephone number. Write the number sentence that you used to get your answer: 0–10, 11–20, 21–30, 31–40.

• Suppose that vowels are worth 6 cents and consonants are worth 7 cents. Determine the value of your first name. Write your name, the number sentence that you used to find this number, and the total on a Post-it and put it on the graph where it belongs: 0–20, 21–40, 41–60, 61–80, 81–100.

CHAPTER 5

Venn Diagrams

I AM WEARING STRIPES

I AM WEARING SHORT SLEEVES

Venn diagrams, or logic rings, are used by teachers to help students think of the ways in which objects or people's characteristics and preferences are alike and different. Our experiences have shown that children find Venn diagrams a wonderful visual organizer of information. On occasion, though, we find that teachers ask for guidance in learning the most effective ways to present Venns to the class. The question most often asked by teachers is, "How can we introduce Venn diagrams to help students get the most from the activity?" Some teachers have said, "We can tell children what the rings mean, but how can we help them without just telling them what the loops are and where to put things?" You'll find our step-by-step tips in this chapter

Introducing Venns

Here is a lesson that we have tried many times. It hasn't failed us yet. We've introduced Venn diagrams to both first and second graders. In all classrooms, children talked about and constructed their own understanding of what to do and why they did it. Then these graphic organizers were used with real understanding by children throughout the grades.

This lesson began after we had been doing various other graphing activities for about three months. The children were "pros" at data collection and, we felt, would welcome a challenge.

We placed two large loops of yarn on the rug of Patti Hughes's classroom. The loops did not overlap, but were only about 6 inches apart at the point where they were closest. The loops were two different colors. They were large enough for many children to sit inside or stand inside. The children stood on the rug around the perimeter of the loops. Honi Bamberger, the consultant for the lesson, had two large rectangular labels which she was about to ask them to read. Before Honi had the children read the labels, she began the lesson as follows:

TEACHER/STUDENT EXCHANGE

Teacher: I want you to look at the rug and think of something that you can say about what I've placed on it.

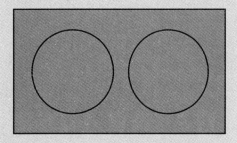

Child: I see two big circles.

Child: One of the circles is green and the other one is yellow.

Child: They are made out of string.

Child: No, they're made out of yarn.

Teacher: I want you to look at one of the labels that I've made for one of the circles. Silently read it. *(Give the children about 10 seconds to read this.)* Who would like to share out loud what the label says?

Child: *(reading):* I am a boy in Ms. Hughes's class.

Teacher: Good! I'm going to put this label right here on the green circle. Now silently read this label. *(Again, give children to do this.)* What does this label say?

Child: *(reading):* I am a girl in Ms. Hughes's class.

Teacher: Good! Now, I'm going to put this label right here on the yellow circle. What do you think I'm going to ask you to do now?

Child: Go inside the circles?

Teacher: Well, actually I'd like you to first think about where you would go. When I say, "GO," I want you to walk over to where you think you belong. *(Honi was standing inside the circle that said, "I am a boy in Ms. Hughes's class." When Honi said "GO," all of the children got up and all of the girls went inside the "girls" circle and all of the boys went inside the "boys" circle.)* How did you know where to go?

Child: The sign said that the girls go here and the boys go there.

Teacher: Look at both of the circles. Is everyone where they're supposed to be?

Child: You're standing in the boys' circle. You're not supposed to be there.

Teacher: I'm not? Where am I supposed to go?

Child: In the girls' circle.

Child: No, she's not a girl. She's a woman.

Teacher: So, where should I go?

Child: You need to stand outside the circles.

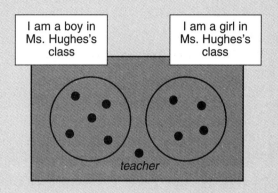

Child: Yeah! You're not a boy in Ms. Hughes's class and you're not a girl in Ms. Hughes's class. So you need to be outside of these circles.

Teacher: But does that still mean that I'm part of the activity?

Children: Yeah!

Teacher: *(Honi stepped outside of the circle.)* Now look at the data that we collected and think of something to say about it. *(Give the children time to think and then have them share their thoughts with a friend, then ask them to share some observations out loud with the group.)* What if I took the label from the girls' circle away and instead put this label on the circle: "I have brown hair." *(Honi had the children read the label silently and then someone read it aloud.)* What do you think will happen?

Child: Some people would need to move.

Teacher: If you think that you need to move somewhere, you may do that now. (*Girls with black and blond hair got up and moved. None of the boys moved.*)

Teacher: How did you know what to do?

Child: Only the people who have brown hair should be in the circle. I have blond hair so I need to be on the outside with you.

Child: But I need to be in the boys' circle and I need to be in the other circle too.

Teacher: So, where do you want to go? If you want to move somewhere, you may.

Child: (*Got up and put one foot in each circle, straddling each.*) I need to be in both because I have brown hair and I'm a boy in Ms. Hughes's class.

Teacher: Is there anyone else who wants to move? (*Two other boys got up, but there was not enough room for all of them to be straddling the two circles.*) What are we going to do?

Child: They could go in the middle between the circles.

Child: No, they can't go there. That would mean that they're not in either circle. That's just like where Dr. Bamberger is standing.

Teacher: So what do we have to do so that everyone who belongs in both circles can fit?

Child: We could do this. (*The student got up and had everyone in both circles move. He then pulled the circles so that they overlapped.*) Then everybody who belongs in both of the circles could stand in here.

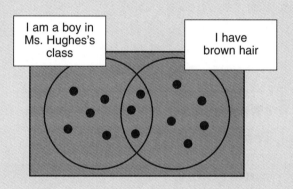

Teacher: So, what does it mean if you're in between?

Child: You have brown hair and you are a boy in Ms. Hughes's class.

Teacher: O.K. Now think about what you might need to do if I moved this label (Honi picked up the boys' label and replaced it with "I am wearing blue jeans.")

This lesson continued until each child said where he/she would stand and why. Then, for the next month, Venn diagrams were used as the organizing device for data collection.

Other Venn Ideas

Here are some other ideas for using Venn diagrams in your first-, second-, third-, and fourth-grade classrooms. (These are suggestions only. Use statements your children will most enjoy.)

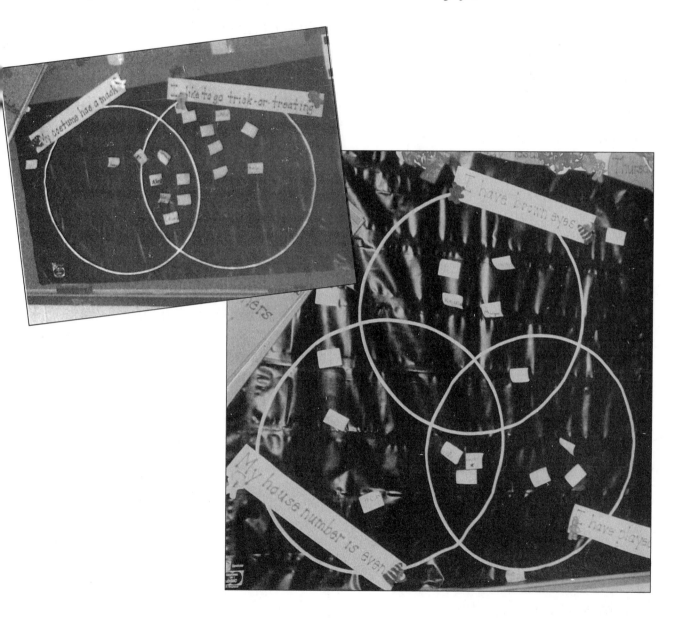

The statements have been sorted by topic, as you may want to present them during social studies, science, or math lessons. Remind children that they may place their answers in one ring only or in spaces shared by two or more rings. Encourage children to talk about the finished diagrams. What conclusions can they draw from their data?

Food

TWO-RING VENNS

- I had cereal for breakfast.
- I had an egg for breakfast.

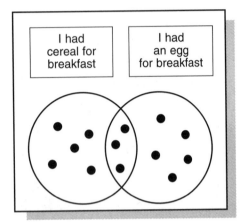

- I like peanut butter-and-jelly sandwiches.
- I can cook dinner for my family.

- I like to eat pretzels.
- I like to eat potato chips.

- I like to eat turkey.
- I like macaroni and cheese.

- I eat one fruit every day.
- I like vegetables.

- I like to drink milk.
- I like orange juice.

- I like thick pizza.
- I like thin pizza.

THREE-RING VENNS

- Breakfast is my favorite meal.
- Lunch is my favorite meal.
- Dinner is my favorite meal.

- I like to eat cookies.
- I like to drink milk.
- I like to eat broccoli.

Names

TWO-RING VENNS

- I have the letter A in my first/last name. (Use any letter.)
- My name begins with the letter ___. (Use any letter.)

- My first/last name has more than five letters in it.
- My first and last names have more than 12 letters in them.

- My first/last name has two different vowels.
- My first/last name begins with a vowel.

- My first/last name begins with a consonant.
- There are more vowels than consonants in my first/last name.

- My name has the letter Q in it.
- My first/last name has two of the same letters in it.

- My name has more consonants than vowels.
- More than half of the letters in my name are consonants.

THREE-RING VENNS
- My name has more than 100 letters in it.
- My first name is longer than my last.
- My last name is longer than my first.

Clothing

TWO-RING VENNS
- I am wearing the color _____ (any color).
- I am wearing stripes.

- I am wearing pants today.
- I wore a coat to school today.

- I am wearing buttons.
- My pants have a zipper.

THREE-RING VENNS
- I am wearing a sweater.
- I am wearing shoes.
- My socks are blue.

- My socks have stripes.
- My shoes have laces.
- My shoes have Velcro.

- I am wearing more than three different colors.
- I am wearing earrings.
- My pants have pockets.

- I wore mittens to school today.
- I wore my boots to school.
- I wore a scarf to school today.

- I am wearing polka dots.
- My clothing has a pattern.
- There are words on my clothing.

Getting To Know You

TWO-RING VENNS
- I like to chew bubble gum.
- I have a brother and a sister.

- I am an only child.
- I am the oldest in my family.

- I like to talk on the phone.
- I like baseball games.

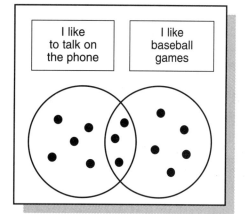

I like to talk on the phone | I like baseball games

- I have more than one brother/sister.
- I have a brother and a sister.

- My hair is long.
- My hair is curly.

- My age is even/odd.
- I am younger than 20.

- My house has a garage.
- My house number is even/odd.

- I have played baseball.
- I play on a sports team.

- My family has a van.
- I have been to Disney World.

THREE-RING VENNS
- I like to swim.
- I know how to drive.
- I like to eat pizza.

- I have pierced ears.
- I wear glasses/contact lenses.
- I can speak another language.

- I am older than 50.
- My birthday is in the summer/spring/fall/winter.
- My favorite color is blue.

- I have been on an airplane.
- I have been to another country.
- I have a pet dog/cat/fish . . .

- I have my own room.
- I like to do homework.
- I would rather read than watch T.V.

- I think school is important.
- I have a computer at home.
- My eyes are green.

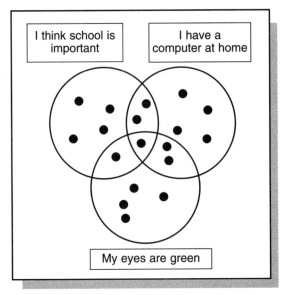

Weather

TWO-RING VENNS
- I like when it rains.
- I have been caught in a thunderstorm.

- I like cold weather.
- I like hot weather.

- My favorite season is fall/winter/spring/summer.
- I heard thunder last night.

- I like when it snows.
- Sunny days are the best.

THREE-RING VENNS
- I have seen a rainbow.
- I like thunderstorms.
- I do not like lightning.

- I have seen hail fall from the sky.
- I like cloudy days.
- I like when the wind whistles.

Holidays

TWO-RING VENNS
- I have a Halloween costume.
- My costume is scary.

- I had a fun Halloween.
- I went trick-or-treating last night.

- My costume has a mask.
- Halloween is my favorite holiday.

- We're going away for Thanksgiving.
- I love celebrating birthdays.

THREE-RING VENNS
- I always wear red on Valentine's Day.
- I stay up past midnight on New Year's Eve.
- I observe some different holidays than my friend.

Numbers

TWO-RING VENNS
- My age plus 10 < 20.
- My birth day is an even number.

- The total number of letters in my first and last name is > 15.
- I was born in a month that comes before June.

- The month of my birthday has less than five letters.
- I can count by twos, fives, and tens to 100.

- The last three digits in my telephone number would make a number that is greater than 500.
- The total of the last three digits of my telephone number is less than 18.

- If A=1, B=2, C=3, D=1, E=2, F=3, G=1 . . . Z and I add up the points for the letters in my first name, the total is greater than 15.
- My age is an even number.

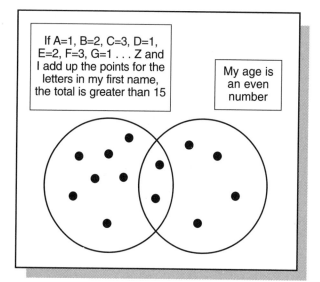

91

- I am wearing a shirt that has an odd number of buttons on it.
- My pants have at least two pockets.

....

- The number of people living with me is greater than four.
- I have at least one pet.

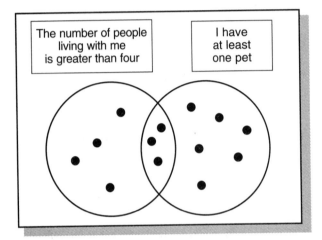

- If I double the last digit of my telephone number it is less than 13.
- If I add five to the last digit of my telephone number it is greater than 9.

....

- In my name there are letters that are doubled (example: Ann).
- The date of my birthday is a double-digit number.

....

- I can name five states in the United States.
- I can name at least three continents in the world.

....

- I have read a book by Beverly Cleary.
- I have read a book by Roald Dahl.

- My favorite kinds of books are chapter books.
- I know how to ride a bicycle.

....

- I can write 5 different three-letter words using the letters in the word MATHEMATICS.
- There are at least two vowels in my first name.

....

- My first name begins with a consonant.
- My last name begins with a consonant.

....

- My first name has more than five consonants in it.
- My first name has only two syllables.

THREE-RING VENNS

- The digit in the ten's place of my address is greater than 4.
- The digit in the one's place of my address is less than 8.
- I have a house number that is greater than 500.

....

- The name of my street has 8 letters or less.
- My address has a name that includes the word *road.*
- My address has a number that is in the thousand's place.

....

- If each button on my clothing was worth 5 cents, my clothing would be worth more than 50 cents.
- If each pocket on my clothing was worth 10 cents, my clothing would be worth more than 50 cents.

- I'm wearing a shirt without a collar.

- In the year 2015 I will be less than 30 years old.
- I know the name of three-sided, four-sided, five-sided, and six-sided shapes.
- I can write 10 letters of the alphabet that have symmetry.

- I can name at least 5 of the 9 planets in the solar system.
- I know the name of the planet that we live on.
- I know how many miles the Earth is from the sun.

- I can name the 12 months in order.
- I can name the 7 days of the week in order.
- I can say the number of minutes in 3 hours.

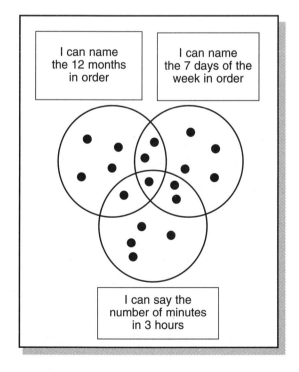

- I know what the Roman numeral CXIX is in our numeration system.
- I can put these fractions in order from the smallest to the largest: 1/5, 5/6, 3/4, 1/4, 1/2.
- I can name three ways that we use fractions in real life.

- I can count to ten in another language besides English.
- My parents speak more than one language.
- I speak more than one language.

- I can unscramble: YPORIBBATLI to make a math word. (Answer: probability)
- I can name the months that have only 30 days.
- I can name the months that have 31 days.

- I have more than $1.00 in my pockets at this time.
- I have more quarters than dimes in my pockets.
- I do not have any pennies in my pockets.

- I have a driver's license.
- I am old enough to drive a car.
- I am always a passenger when I am in a car.

- My age is the same number as my shoe size.
- There is a coin that is worth the same number as my age.
- I usually keep my money in a bank.

CHAPTER 6

Glyphs

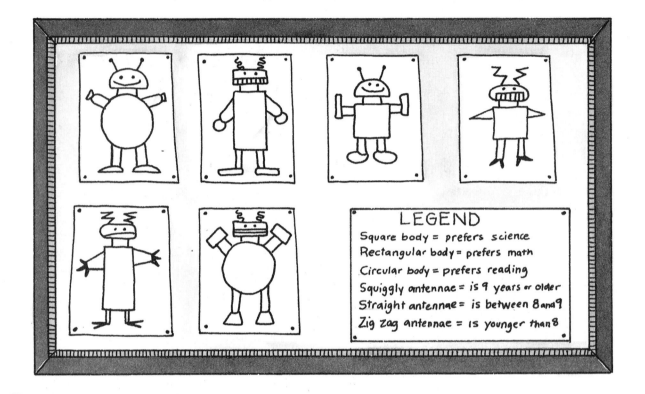

What is a Glyph? Just as a graph is a chart that conveys information, a glyph—short for hieroglyphics—is a form of picture writing that conveys information. To make a glyph in the classroom, data is collected, a legend is created, and specific components of the final picture have significance. In classroom use, the legend explains what each feature of the glyph represents. The individual features of the finished glyph tell a story about the person who created it. In the robot glyphs shown here, two children prefer science, and two more prefer math. Two children are between eight and nine years old, two are younger than eight, and two are nine years or older. Can you tell who they are?

Introducing Apple Glyphs

MATERIALS/DIRECTIONS

Cut out a large red apple from construction paper. Position the stem so it points to the right. Put three green leaves on the stem, and a worm sticking out of a place at the bottom of the apple. Show this to the class.

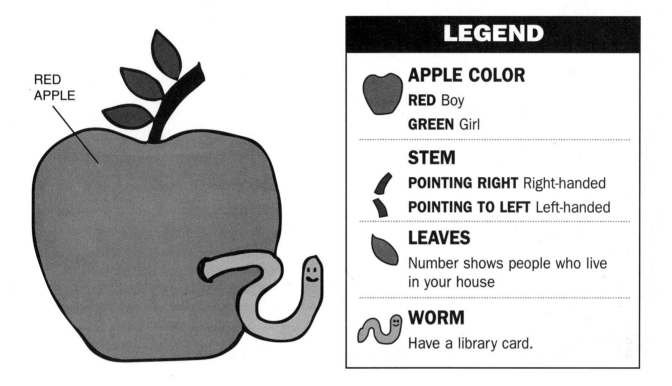

RED APPLE

LEGEND

APPLE COLOR
RED Boy
GREEN Girl

STEM
POINTING RIGHT Right-handed
POINTING TO LEFT Left-handed

LEAVES
Number shows people who live in your house

WORM
Have a library card.

TEACHER/STUDENT EXCHANGE

Teacher: Class, please look at the picture and think of something that you can say. Whisper to a friend what you were thinking. Who would like to share something that you heard or were thinking?

Child: I see an apple.

Child: The apple is red.

Child: There's a worm inside the apple.

Child: Part of the worm is sticking out.

Child: No one has taken a bite out of the apple.

Teacher: How do you know that?

Child: It's still smooth all around.

Child: The apple has a stem.

Child: The stem is brown and it's pointing to the right.

Child: There are three leaves on the stem.

Teacher: This picture of an apple means something. This chart is called a *legend* and it tells us what each part of the apple means. Look at the chart and read what it says. (*Give students time to do this.*) Raise your hand if you would like to read what the color of the apple means.

Child: The color of the apple shows if you are a boy or a girl. If it's red, it means you are a boy. If it's green, it means that you are a girl.

Teacher: So, looking at the picture, is the artist a girl or a boy? (*Have a child answer and then go on to the next feature of the glyph.*)

Teacher: What does the next part of this picture tell us?

Child: The way that the stem is pointing tells whether you use your right hand or your left hand to write. If the stem points to the right, you are right-handed. If the stem points to the left, you're left-handed.

Teacher: Is the artist of the apple right-handed or left-handed? How do you know?

Teacher: What does the next part of this picture tell us?

Child: The number of leaves means how many people live in your house. Since there are only three leaves on the picture that means that three people live in this person's house.

Teacher: And what does the worm mean?

Child: If there is a worm poking out of the apple, it means that you have a library card. If there isn't a worm it means that you don't have a library card.

Teacher: So, does the person who made this picture have a library card?

Children: Yes!

Teacher: This is a very special kind of a picture. It's called a *glyph.* (*Write the word on chart paper or on the overhead projector.*) It comes from the word *hieroglyphics.* (*Write this word.*) How are these words alike? (*Discuss.*) In ancient times, stories were told on the walls of caves using pictures. These pictures were called hieroglyphics. Our glyphs also tell us stories. They provide information about ourselves.

We are each going to make an apple glyph today. These apple glyphs will tell us information about whether we are a boy or a girl, whether we have a library card, which hand we use to write, and how many people live in our house. You will need to glue your apple onto construction paper and then make each part of your glyph so that the information you are telling is true. (*Have large red and green apples already cut out so that children only need to cut out a stem, leaves, and a worm.*)

Then have children talk about:
- how many girls there are in the class.
- how many people have a library card.
- how many people write with their left hand.
- how many people write with their right hand.
- how many people live with two, three, four, five, . . . people.

You might use some other graphic organizers (tally, bar graph, chart, or table) to display this information. Or you may choose to just discuss this data without recording it.

Once all of the students have created glyphs, the glyphs become part of the class's data. Children—in pairs or groups—can focus on specific components of the glyphs, and determine a way to represent, analyze, and interpret the information.

Special Glyphs

Holidays, seasonal events, and theme units are ideal motivators for creating eye-catching glyphs. The first ten projects that follow are appropriate for nearly every month of the year, from September to June. (For May, let your students suggest a glyph.) The last three projects correlate well to special curriculum units, such as shelter, and are appropriate for most months of the year. Some of the glyphs convey personal information about youngsters. Feel free to change these to less personal information, if you prefer.

Snowperson

Umbrella

House

Leprechaun

Valentine

Earth Day

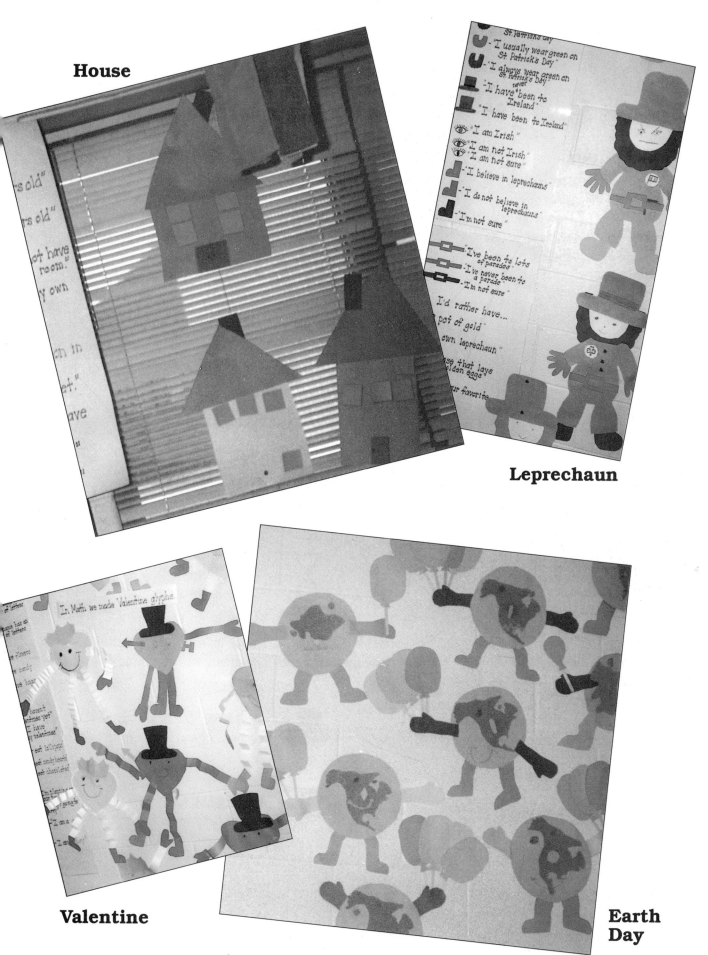

Face It, We're Cute!

MATERIALS

- paper plate (face)
- yarn (hair)
- crayons (to draw mouth, eyes, nose, freckles)
- paste or glue
- scissors

BASEBALL CAP: Name starts with M

BLUE HAIR: Birthday in April

BLACK EYES: Likes reading

TRIANGLE NOSE: Lives in a house

MOUTH: Has a brother

FOUR FRECKLES: Name is Mary

LEGEND

HAIR

"My birthday is in. . .

BLUE January, February, March or April."

RED May, June, July or August."

YELLOW September, October, November or December."

EYES

BLACK "I like reading the most."

BLUE "I like math the most."

BROWN "I like science the most."

GREEN "I like social studies the most."

FRECKLES

1 freckle for each letter in your first name

MOUTH

"I only have a brother."

"I only have a sister."

"I have both brother(s) and sister(s)."

"I am an only child."

NOSE

"I live in a house."

"I live in a townhouse."

"I live in an apartment."

"I live in a different home."

HAT

TOP HAT "My first name begins with a letter from A to J."

BASEBALL CAP "My first name begins with a letter from K to Z."

Halloween

MATERIALS

- paper plate (pumpkin)
- crayons (for eyes, nose, mouth)
- construction paper (for stem and leaves)
- paste or glue
- scissors

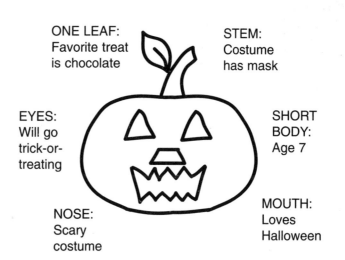

ONE LEAF:
Favorite treat is chocolate

STEM:
Costume has mask

EYES:
Will go trick-or-treating

SHORT BODY:
Age 7

NOSE:
Scary costume

MOUTH:
Loves Halloween

LEGEND

BODY

TALL "My age is an even number."

SHORT "My age is an odd number."

EYES

"On Halloween. . .

I will go trick-or-treating."

I will go to a party."

I will stay home."

NOSE

"My costume. . .

is scary."

is funny."

is a T.V./movie/story character."

hasn't been decided yet."

STEM

TO THE RIGHT "My costume has a mask."

TO THE LEFT "My costume does not have a mask."

MOUTH

"I like Halloween."

"I love Halloween."

"I do not like Halloween."

LEAVES

"My favorite Halloween treat. . .

ONE is chocolate."

TWO are lollipops."

THREE is bubble gum."

Turkey

MATERIALS

- construction paper (body, feet, beak, wattle)
- crayons (feathers, eyes)
- paste or glue
- scissors

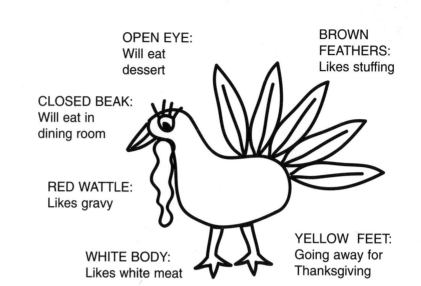

OPEN EYE:
Will eat dessert

BROWN FEATHERS:
Likes stuffing

CLOSED BEAK:
Will eat in dining room

RED WATTLE:
Likes gravy

WHITE BODY:
Likes white meat

YELLOW FEET:
Going away for Thanksgiving

LEGEND

BODY

DARK BROWN "I like dark meat."

LIGHT BROWN "I like white meat."

WHITE "I don't eat turkey."

FEET

YELLOW "I am going away for Thanksgiving."

RED "I am not going away for Thanksgiving."

BEAK

"On Thanksgiving we usually eat in the. . .

OPENED kitchen."

CLOSED dining room."

WATTLE

RED "I like gravy."

ORANGE "I do not like gravy."

FEATHERS

"On Thanksgiving I like to eat. . .

RED cranberries."

ORANGE pumpkin pie."

GREEN green beans."

YELLOW corn."

BROWN stuffing."

PINK mashed potatoes."

EYES

OPENED "I will eat dessert on Thanksgiving."

CLOSED "I will not eat dessert on Thanksgiving."

Reindeer

MATERIALS

- construction paper (body, antlers, tail, legs)
- crayons (eyes, neck decoration, nose)
- paste or glue
- scissors

ANTLERS: Six years old

EYES TO RIGHT: Loves to read

GREEN NOSE: A boy

BOW: Not going away for holidays

TAIL UP: Favorite season is winter

1 BENT LEG: The youngest child

LEGEND

ANTLERS

Number of prongs tells your age.

"I am six."

"I am seven."

EYES

LOOKING RIGHT "I love to read."

LOOKING LEFT "I like to read."

STRAIGHT AHEAD "I do not like to read."

NECK DECORATION

Vacation plans

BELL "I am going away for the holidays."

BOW "I am not going away for the holidays."

NOSE

GREEN "I am a boy."

RED "I am a girl."

TAIL

"My favorite season is. . .

UP winter."

DOWN spring."

RIGHT summer."

LEFT fall."

LEGS

1 BENT LEG "I am the youngest child."

2 BENT LEGS "I am the oldest child."

3 BENT LEGS "I am in the middle."

4 BENT LEGS "I am the only child."

Snowperson

MATERIALS

- construction paper (body, clothing, broom/shovel)
- crayons (mouth)
- paste or glue
- scissors

SCARF: Winter not favorite season

MOUTH: Likes soup

EAR MUFFS: Girl

MITTENS: Wears mittens to keep warm

TRIANGLE BUTTONS: Close school when it snows

RED BOOTS: Likes building forts in winter

BROOM: Likes snow

LEGEND

HEAD COVERING

EAR MUFFS
"I am a girl."

SKI CAP
"I am a boy."

MOUTH

"On a cold day, I'd rather. . .

drink hot chocolate."

eat soup."

have something else."

MITTENS/GLOVES

"In winter, I'd rather. . .

wear mittens to keep my hands warm."

wear gloves to keep my hands warm."

BOOTS

"In winter, I'd rather. . .

PURPLE go sledding."

RED build forts."

BLUE throw snowballs."

BUTTONS

"When it snows, it's best when school. . .

TRIANGLE is closed."

CIRCLE has delayed openings."

SQUARE closes early."

SCARF

"Winter is. . .

SOLID my favorite season."

STRIPED not my favorite season."

BROOM/SHOVEL

BROOM
"I like snow."

SHOVEL
"I don't like snow."

Valentine

MATERIALS

- construction paper (body, head, clothing, arms/legs)
- crayons (decoration)
- paste or glue
- scissors

PINK BODY: Valentine's Day is OK

ARROW: Boy

CROWN: Name has even number of letters

RED MITTENS: Prefers candy for gift

STRAIGHT ARMS: Valentines are written

FOLDED LEGS: Will wear red on Valentine's day

PURPLE BOOTS: Prefers chocolate

LEGEND

BODY/HEAD

PINK "Valentine's Day is okay."

RED "Valentine's Day is not my favorite holiday."

PURPLE "Valentine's Day is my favorite holiday."

HAT

TOP HAT "My first name has an odd number of letters in it."

CROWN "My first name has an even number of letters in it."

MITTENS

BLUE "I'd rather have flowers for a gift."

RED "I'd rather have candy for a gift."

PURPLE "I'd rather have hugs for a gift."

ARMS

FOLDED "I haven't written my valentines yet."

STRAIGHT "I have written my valentines."

BOOTS

BLUE "I'd rather eat lollipops."

RED "I'd rather eat candy hearts."

PURPLE I'd rather eat chocolates."

LEGS

FOLDED "I'm planning to wear red on Valentine's Day."

STRAIGHT "I'm not going to wear red on Valentine's Day."

DECORATION

LACE AROUND BODY "I am a girl."

ARROW THROUGH BODY "I am a boy."

Leprechaun

MATERIALS

- construction paper (body, clothing)
- crayons (eyes)
- paste or glue
- scissors

HAT: Never been to Ireland

ORANGE BEARD: Always wear green

BROWN EYES: Not Irish

RED GLOVES: Prefers a pot of gold

RED BELT: Been to many parades

RED BOOTS: Believes in leprechauns

LEGEND

BEARD

"On St. Patrick's Day. . .

BLACK I never wear green."

BROWN I usually wear green."

ORANGE I always wear green."

GLOVES

RED "I'd rather have a pot of gold."

BLUE "I'd rather have my own leprechaun."

BLACK "I'd rather have a goose that lays golden eggs.

EYES

BLUE "I am Irish."

GREEN "I am part Irish."

BROWN "I am not Irish."

BLACK "I am not sure."

BOOTS

RED "I believe in leprechauns."

BLUE "I do not believe in leprechauns."

BLACK "I'm not sure."

HAT

"I have never been to Ireland."

"I have been to Ireland."

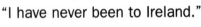

BELT

RED "I've been to many parades."

BLUE "I've been to a few parades."

BLACK "I've never been to a parade."

BUTTON

Choose the one that you like:

shamrock

Ireland's flag

"Kiss me I'm Irish"

Umbrella

MATERIALS

- construction paper (umbrella shape, handle, tag)
- crayons (umbrella design)
- yarn (cord for carrying)
- stickers (handle decorations)

SHAPE: Likes rainy days

LAST NAME ON TAG: Not going away

EGG STICKERS: Likes thunderstorms

STRIPES: Liked when Roger's umbrella carried him away

HANDLE TO RIGHT: Spring not favorite season

RED CORD: Likes roses

HANDLE SHAPE: Reads on rainy days

LEGEND

SHAPE

"I love rainy days."

"I like rainy days."

"I do not like rainy days."

HANDLE

"On rainy days, I'd rather. . .

 read."

play a game."

watch T.V."

HANDLE DIRECTION

TO THE LEFT "Spring is my favorite season."

TO THE RIGHT "Spring is not my favorite season."

TAG FOR NAME

FIRST NAME "I am going away for Spring Break."

LAST NAME "I am not going away for Spring Break."

CORD FOR CARRYING

RED "I like roses."

PURPLE "I like tulips."

YELLOW "I like daisies."

UMBRELLA DESIGN

We read *Roger's Umbrella* and answered this:

"I liked when. . .

STRIPED Roger's umbrella carried him away."

PLAID Roger's umbrella flew like a bat."

FLOWERED the ladies taught Roger how to talk to his umbrella."

HANDLE DECORATIONS

Any mini stickers will do for this:

STRIPED EGG STICKERS "I like thunderstorms."

BUNNY STICKERS "I do not like thunderstorms."

Earth Day

MATERIALS

- construction paper (globe shape, continents, balloons, arms, legs)
- crayons (for mouth, eyes)
- paste or glue
- scissors

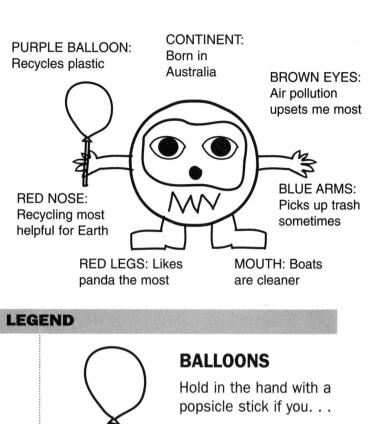

PURPLE BALLOON: Recycles plastic

CONTINENT: Born in Australia

BROWN EYES: Air pollution upsets me most

RED NOSE: Recycling most helpful for Earth

BLUE ARMS: Picks up trash sometimes

RED LEGS: Likes panda the most

MOUTH: Boats are cleaner

LEGEND

GLOBE

Everybody should start with a circle.

CONTINENT

Paste on the globe. Choose the continent where you were born.

 Asia

Antarctica

Europe

North America

South America

Africa

 Australia

BALLOONS

Hold in the hand with a popsicle stick if you. . .

RED recycle aluminum cans.

YELLOW recycle news-papers.

PURPLE recycle plastic.

BLUE recycle glass.

ARMS

YELLOW "I pick up trash all the time."

BLUE "I pick up trash sometimes."

RED "I never pick up trash."

MOUTH

"What's the cleanest form of transportation?"

trains

airplanes

boats

cars

LEGS

"Which endangered animal do you like the most?"

RED panda

YELLOW tiger

BLUE blue whale

EYES

"Which type of pollution upsets you the most?"

BROWN air

BLUE noise

GREEN water

BLACK soil/ground

NOSE

"What's the most helpful thing that you can do to help save the Earth?"

RED recycle

BLUE conserve energy

GREEN use less water

YELLOW plant a tree

Boats

GREAT FOR June

MATERIALS

- construction paper (boat shape, portholes, sails, mast, flag, sail decoration, anchor)
- paste or glue
- scissors

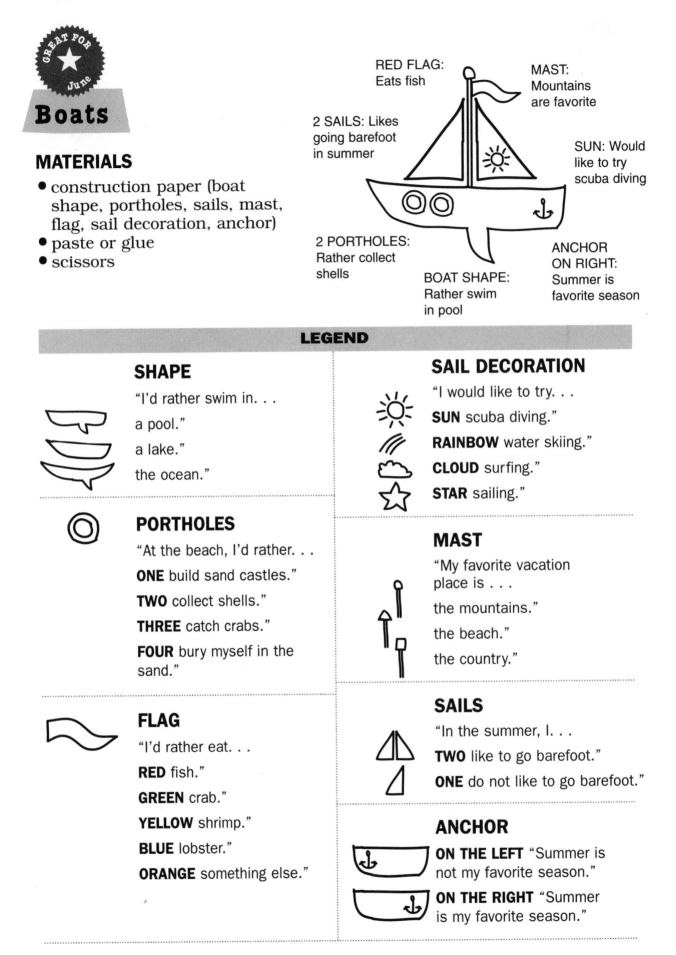

RED FLAG: Eats fish

MAST: Mountains are favorite

2 SAILS: Likes going barefoot in summer

SUN: Would like to try scuba diving

2 PORTHOLES: Rather collect shells

BOAT SHAPE: Rather swim in pool

ANCHOR ON RIGHT: Summer is favorite season

LEGEND

SHAPE

"I'd rather swim in. . .

a pool."

a lake."

the ocean."

PORTHOLES

"At the beach, I'd rather. . .

ONE build sand castles."

TWO collect shells."

THREE catch crabs."

FOUR bury myself in the sand."

FLAG

"I'd rather eat. . .

RED fish."

GREEN crab."

YELLOW shrimp."

BLUE lobster."

ORANGE something else."

SAIL DECORATION

"I would like to try. . .

SUN scuba diving."

RAINBOW water skiing."

CLOUD surfing."

STAR sailing."

MAST

"My favorite vacation place is . . .

the mountains."

the beach."

the country."

SAILS

"In the summer, I. . .

TWO like to go barefoot."

ONE do not like to go barefoot."

ANCHOR

ON THE LEFT "Summer is not my favorite season."

ON THE RIGHT "Summer is my favorite season."

GREAT FOR Shelter Unit

House

MATERIALS

- construction paper (house shape, roog, windows, door, chimney, path)
- crayons
- paste or glue
- scissors

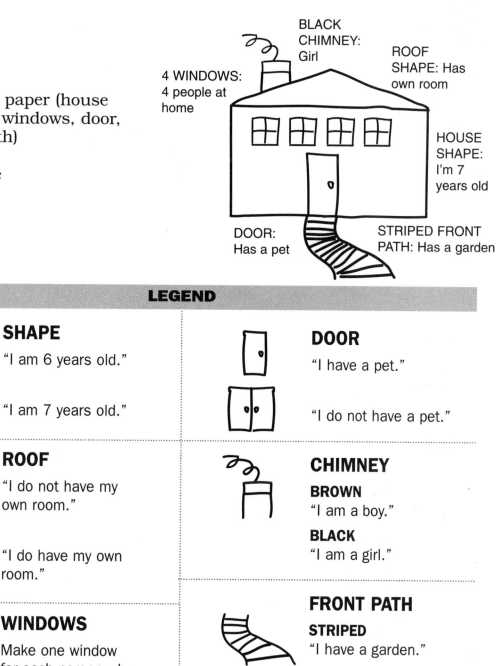

BLACK CHIMNEY: Girl

ROOF SHAPE: Has own room

4 WINDOWS: 4 people at home

HOUSE SHAPE: I'm 7 years old

DOOR: Has a pet

STRIPED FRONT PATH: Has a garden

LEGEND

SHAPE

"I am 6 years old."

"I am 7 years old."

ROOF

"I do not have my own room."

"I do have my own room."

WINDOWS

Make one window for each person who lives in your house.

DOOR

"I have a pet."

"I do not have a pet."

CHIMNEY

BROWN
"I am a boy."

BLACK
"I am a girl."

FRONT PATH

STRIPED
"I have a garden."

PLAIN
"I don't have a garden."

Watch

Older students enjoy making glyphs that convey lots of information. This "designer-watch" glyph not only gives children an opportunity to connect their knowledge about time with their understanding of time given months of the year, but it's visually appealing and motivating as well. Stencils can be made for the watch face and the bands so that some consistency exists. In addition, excess time isn't spent on the early stages of the activity.

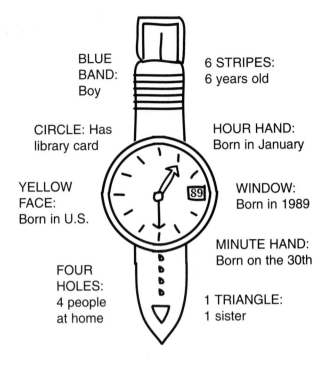

BLUE BAND: Boy

CIRCLE: Has library card

YELLOW FACE: Born in U.S.

FOUR HOLES: 4 people at home

6 STRIPES: 6 years old

HOUR HAND: Born in January

WINDOW: Born in 1989

MINUTE HAND: Born on the 30th

1 TRIANGLE: 1 sister

MATERIALS

- construction paper (watch face, band)
- crayons (circle, hands, decorations, stripes)
- paste or glue
- scissors

BAND COLOR

The color of the band represents male and female.

MALE blue

FEMALE green

WATCH HANDS

The hour hand points to the numeral that shows the month that you were born.

The minute hand points to the place on the clock that shows the day (date) that you were born.
EXAMPLE: 22nd
22 minutes after

[89] The small "window" on the right side of the clock face shows the year (only ten's and one's places) that you were born. This is where the date usually is on a watch.

WATCHBAND

The number of holes on the watchband shows how many people live with you in your home.

CLOCK FACE COLOR

The color of the clock face represents where you were born.

YELLOW in the United States

ORANGE outside the United States

DECORATIONS

▽ Red triangles on the band represent the number of sisters you have.

○ Purple circles on the band represent the number of brothers you have.

STRIPES

Stripes on the band represent your age in years.

CIRCLE

Place a circle around the circumference of the clock face if you have a library card.

No circle means that you do not have a library card.

Lunch Box

MATERIALS

- construction paper (container, sandwich, fruit, napkin, drink, ice cream)
- paste or glue
- scissors

LUNCH BOX: Rather have hot dog

NAPKIN: Always buys lunch

APPLE: First name has less than 5 letters

WHITE DRINK: Likes milk

ICE CREAM: Rather eat ice-cream cup

BROWN SANDWICH: Likes wheat bread

LEGEND

CONTAINER

"For lunch I'd rather have. . .

LUNCH BOX a hot dog."

A BAG a hamburger."

A TRAY a grilled cheese."

SANDWICH

"I like. . .

BROWN wheat bread."

WHITE white bread."

FRUIT

The word "fruit" has five letters.

GRAPES "My first name has 5 letters."

BANANA "My first name has more than 5 letters."

APPLE "My first name has less than 5 letters."

NAPKIN

Use 3 different styles of real napkins.

"At school. . .

I always buy lunch."

I sometimes buy lunch."

I never buy lunch."

DRINK

"My favorite kind of milk is. . .

BROWN chocolate milk."

WHITE white milk."

PINK strawberry milk."

ICE CREAM

"I'd rather eat. . .

a popsicle."

an ice-cream sandwich."

an ice-cream cup."

Basic Supply List

Use this handy checklist to assemble the materials needed to make the graphs, venns, and glyphs in the book.

- [ ] adhesive dots, various colors
- [ ] 2-liter soda bottles
- [ ] bucket
- [ ] clothespins
- [ ] connecting cubes
- [ ] construction paper
- [ ] containers of various sizes
- [ ] crayons
- [ ] food coloring
- [ ] funnel
- [ ] hula hoops
- [ ] index cards (assorted colors)
- [ ] laminated bulletin board paper
- [ ] chalkboard compass
- [ ] markers (permanent and write on/wipe off)
- [ ] masking tape
- [ ] measuring cup
- [ ] milk containers, empty and washed

- [ ] multicolored Post-it notes
- [ ] oil cloth
- [ ] paper
- [ ] paper clips
- [ ] paper fasteners
- [ ] paste or glue
- [ ] pencils
- [ ] photographs of your students
- [ ] pictures from discarded magazines
- [ ] poster board
- [ ] scissors
- [ ] scoop
- [ ] sentence strips
- [ ] shower curtain liners
- [ ] string/yarn
- [ ] transparent vinyl (available at fabric stores)
- [ ] Velcro
- [ ] window shades
- [ ] yardstick or meterstick

Useful Pictures

Copy and cut out these pictures to use with some of the graphs, Venns, and glyphs in the book.

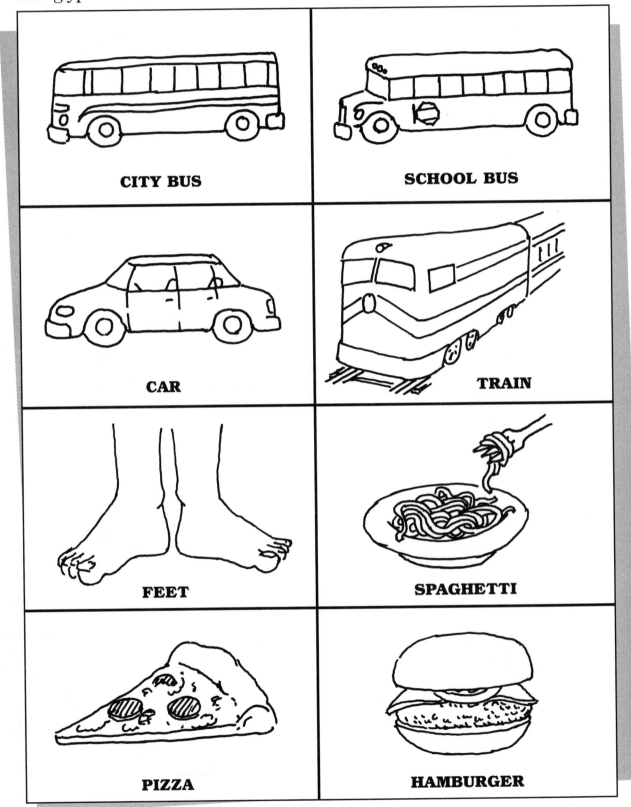

CITY BUS

SCHOOL BUS

CAR

TRAIN

FEET

SPAGHETTI

PIZZA

HAMBURGER

Useful Pictures

LION

TIGER

DOCTOR

TEACHER

PARENT

CAT

DOG

HORSE

Grid Paper

You may want to adapt some of the graph ideas in the book for students to use individually. If so, you may find this grid paper useful for this purpose.

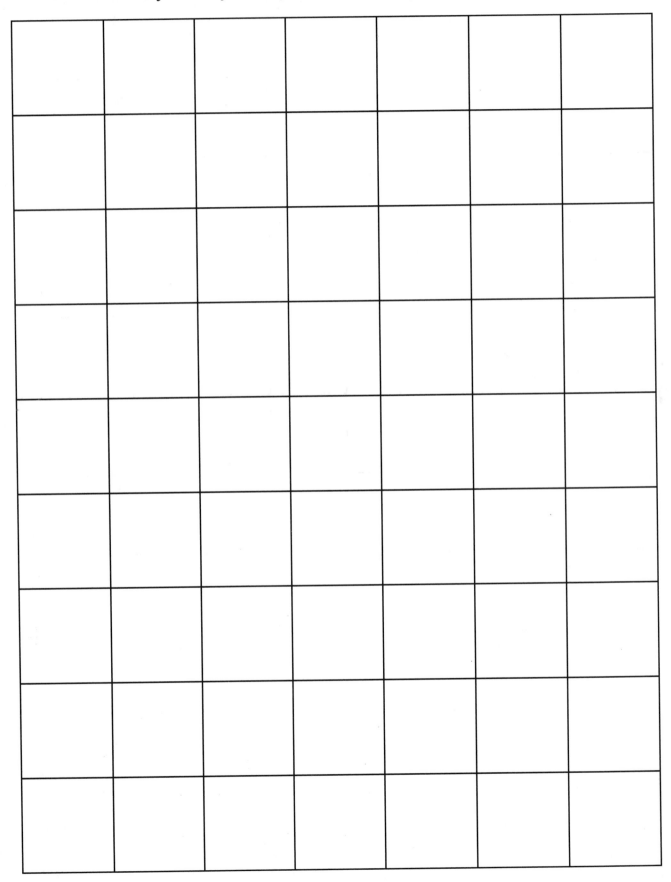

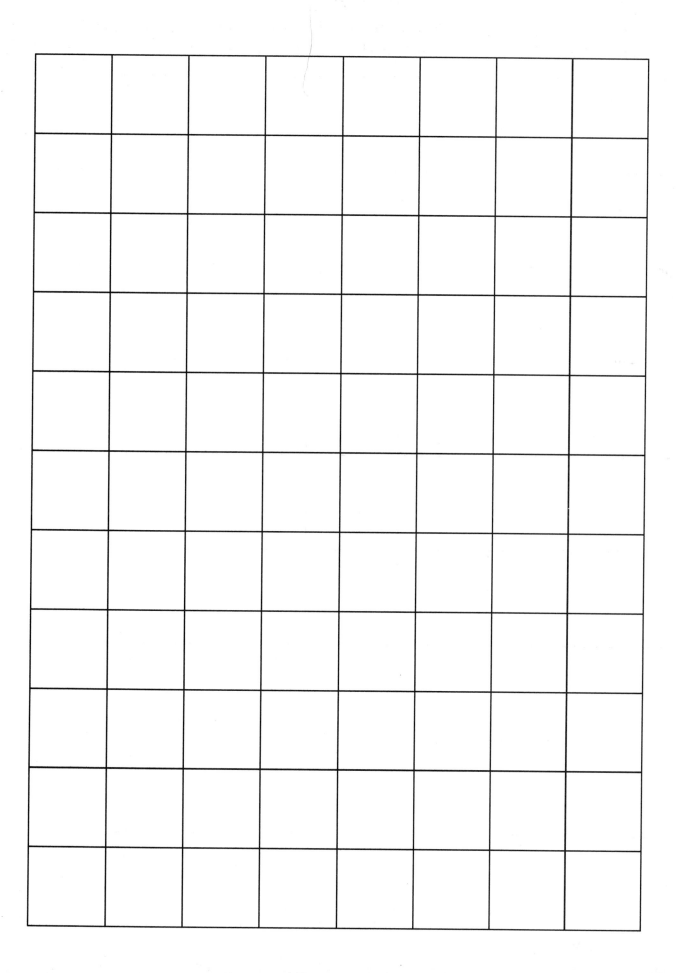

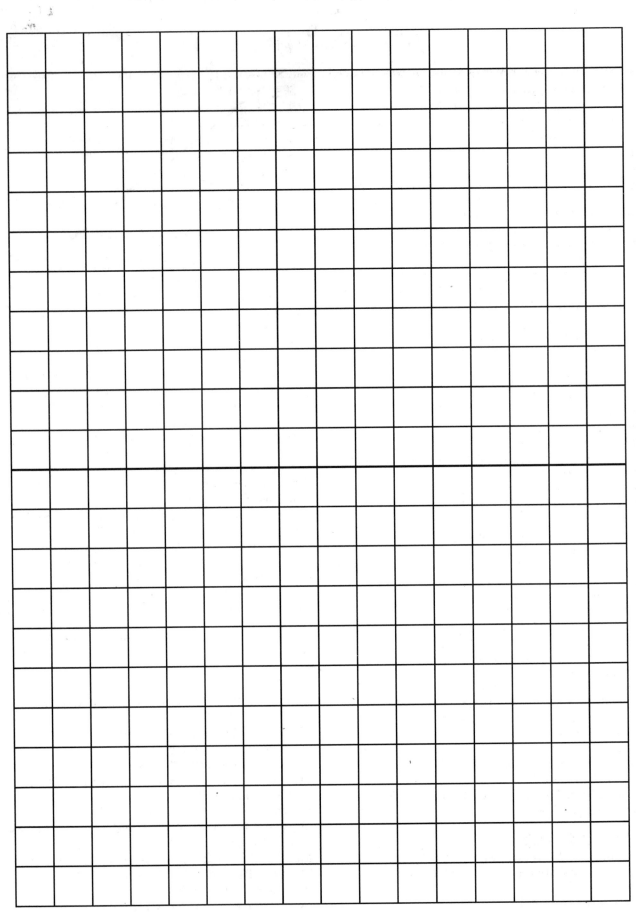